Praise for Anne Newton Walther's book
DIVORCE HANGOVER: A Successful Strategy to End the Emotional Aftermath of Divorce,
the companion volume to *NOT DAMAGED GOODS*

"A step-by-step path to mental equilibrium, *DIVORCE HANGOVER* touts positive thinking, self-reliance, conflict resolution and a determined effort to create financial and emotional independence."
—*Atlanta Journal-Constitution*

"Liberating . . . ."
—*Dallas Morning News*

"an eminently practical approach that is 'guaranteed to work.'"
—*Rochester Times-Union*

"There's a lot of help out there for divorced people in the way of books . . . [but] the best book I've seen in a long time is *DIVORCE HANGOVER.*"
—*Star* (Tarrytown, NY)

"Many books have been written . . . about divorce . . . , but what's been needed . . . is something really worthwhile on 'after divorce.' Now we've got one and a good one. *DIVORCE HANGOVER* is it. . . . We desperately need the practical, valuable, down-to-earth and human advice that Anne Walther doles out."

—Melvin M. Belli
Attorney

"Anne Walther describes in this book a devastating syndrome that she aptly designates 'divorce hangover.' . . . [She delineates] the possible causes and all the symptoms of this chronic illness, . . . [and] presents in a simple but magisterial manner precisely the steps one can take either to avoid or to rid oneself of this emotionally crippling disorder. This book may well be one of the monumental psychological books of this decade. Certainly it should be on the 'must read' list not only of men and women already suffering from 'divorce hangover' but also by those who may be contemplating divorce."

—Meyer Friedman, M.D.
Mount Zion Medical Center,
University of California, San Francisco

"*DIVORCE HANGOVER* is filled with excellent advice and workbook exercises that every divorced person will find truly helpful. It is a very readable, caring book that demonstrates clearly and concisely how you can dispel the divorce hangover demons from your life."

—Mel Krantzler, Ph.D.
Director of the Creative Divorce,
Love and Marriage Counseling Center

NOT DAMAGED GOODS

ALSO BY ANNE NEWTON WALTHER

Divorce Hangover: A Successful Strategy to End the Emotional Aftermath of Divorce
(TAPESTRIES PUBLISHING)

A Time for Treason: A Novel of the American Revolution
(TAPESTRIES PUBLISHING)

NOT DAMAGED GOODS

A Successful Strategy for Children of Divorce from Infancy to Adulthood

Anne Newton Walther, M.S.

TAPESTRIES PUBLISHING :: SAN FRANCISCO

Original trade paperback published by
TAPESTRIES PUBLISHING
www.tapestriespublishing.com
Distributed by IPM, 800-758-3756

Library of Congress Control Number 2001131578

Publisher's Cataloging-in-Publication Data
Walther, Anne Newton.
Not damaged goods : a successful strategy for children of divorce from infancy to adulthood / Anne Newton Walther, M.S.
p. cm.
ISBN 0-9676703-2-2
1. Children of divorced parents—United States. 2. Adult children of divorced parents—Psychology. 3. Adult children of divorced parents—Attitudes. 4. Adult children of divorced parents—Mental Health. 5. Divorce—United States. I. Title.

306.89—dc21 2001131578

Cover and text design: George Mattingly Design/Berkeley

Printing and binding: Data Reproductions Corp.

Printed on acid-free paper

ISBN 0-9676703-2-2

To my children:

To Jad and Beau,
who have been with me from the beginning

To Wendy, Christy, and Ted,
who entered my life with my second marriage

You five,
each of you a sparkling star,
and each a veteran of the experience

Contents

Part Three
Developmental Stages and Divorce for Ages 20 and Up

Acknowledgments

Thank you, Beau, for your knowledge of contemporary music and your inspired suggestions of lyrics for chapter titles. Thank you, Zipporah, Alice, and Kathleen, the architect, the voice, and the network, for making this book a reality.

To every child, of whatever age, who has weathered the storm of his or her parents' divorce, and survived, prevailed, and prospered, I salute you.

Preface

"Guess what? Mom and Dad are getting a divorce!" My son, age 6, made that announcement during "show and tell" to his first-grade class in 1975 with all the flourish of pulling a rabbit out of a hat. Divorce carried no stigma for him. He didn't know he was supposed to feel bad, so he didn't. My ex-husband and I surrounded him with people who supported his "What, me worry?" point of view and worked out as normal a routine as possible for our 6-year-old little boy. He had his share of scraped knees (with a broken wrist thrown in for good measure), school prizes, teenage experimentation, and happy compatriots. Somewhere along the way he grew up. Jad's now 33 years old, with an intact psyche and a healthy dose of ambition, and is living happily with his wife, Christina, and his 1-year-old son, Mason.

On the surface, Chris Zorich's childhood was very different from my son's. He was beaten up probably a hundred times growing up in a Chicago southeast-side ghetto. There was no father to defend him, only a diabetic mother, Zorka Zorich. The sole support for Zorka and her son was her monthly $200 welfare disability check. But her devotion to him was unrelenting; his daily creed was her words, "Things are going to get better." His neighborhood didn't sport gyms and health clubs.

He bulked up using manhole covers and lifting bars stuck between two sewer lids.

He graduated from Notre Dame University, where he had been the starting noseguard for "The Fighting Irish" and the winner of the Lombardi Trophy. Chris went on to play professional football for the Chicago Bears.

During his childhood, the love and devotion that he and his mother shared were legendary. Not all children are as lucky as Chris to have a mother whose optimistic conviction and unqualified love for her son transformed his desperate circumstances into self-respect and personal motivation.

But all children do have the birthright of childhood. Are children raised by divorced parents or in single-parent families in a separate category marked "damaged goods"? No, not if they are given the necessary tools to handle these circumstances.

Not Damaged Goods answers that need. It gives children of divorce the chance to help themselves. It is the first book to show that divorce can be an opportunity for growth and self-understanding, instead of being a permanent, emotional setback. It is the first book that helps readers understand that the divorce experience affects the young person's whole life span and that it must be handled in just that way if its aftermath is to be treated effectively. With this book, the reader can deal with the painful issues of divorce as they occur at each age and stage of development, instead of artificially confining the divorce experience to the time when the divorce occurred.

This book's unique format, which incorporates the stages from early childhood up through adulthood, offers young people the ability to assess the effects of divorce on them prior to their current age, understand the issues they and their contemporaries are presently facing, and anticipate the challenges that they will confront in the future.

With the help of the chapters' "dialogues," the young people recognize that their own painful issues are common to all children dealing with their parents' divorce. They can come to terms with the issues, understand the feelings they cause, and build self-esteem as they take pride in sorting through this experience without suffering long-term consequences.

Part One

Developmental Stages and Divorce for Ages 1–12

Chapter 1

Infancy Through Kindergarten

(AGES 0–5)

"Once upon a Time"

Instructions

This chapter is designed for you the parent to use with your child or children. As parent, you should first read the chapter all the way through and then use the exercise or exercises best suited for the child to help him or her deal with fears and anxieties.

For Children Ages 0–2

Use toys or stuffed animals to demonstrate different feelings, such as love, joy, crankiness, fear, happiness, and so on.

Examples

"Teddy Bear is happy because he just had a bowl of honey."
"Teddy Bear is sad because he had to stay inside all day."
"Teddy Bear is warm and cozy because he just had a nice, warm bath and lots of hugs from Mommy Bear."

"Teddy Bear is scared because Mommy and Daddy Bear are growling at each other, but hugs and kisses from Mommy and Daddy Bear make the scary feelings go away."

Make up more Teddy Bear feelings. Make up conversations with Teddy Bear and other stuffed animals, and conduct them with your child.

For Children Ages 3–5

The Story

Once upon a time there was a little brown house nestled in the trees at the edge of a forest. In the house lived a very pretty Mommy and a handsome Daddy and two little children, named Michael and Elizabeth.

On days that were sunny, Mommy took Michael and Elizabeth for walks in the woods. Mommy showed them the squirrels running up in the trees carrying nuts in their mouths.

Mommy was always careful not to step on the beautiful wild flowers. She named each one and taught Elizabeth and Michael to love the plants and trees and to name them as they walked by. Michael and Elizabeth especially loved the butterflies. The monarchs were Elizabeth's favorite, but Michael liked the swallowtails the best.

The children loved the smells of the forest, the earth, the moss, the plants, and trees. They listened to the voices of the forest, too: the chirping of the birds, the gurgling of the brook, the wind through the leaves, the skittering sounds of little furry animals.

On rainy days, Michael and Elizabeth helped Mommy bake and clean. Sometimes there was even time to read a story together by the fireplace before Daddy came home.

The best time of the day was when Daddy walked through the door, smiling and calling, "Where are my two favorite children in the whole world?" Then Michael and Elizabeth would dash out from wherever they were playing and jump up and down, telling Daddy all the exciting things that had happened.

Daddy and Mommy always gave each other a special hug and kiss. Then, smiling at one another and holding hands, they sat in the living room and talked quietly together until everyone got up and put dinner on the table.

Michael and Elizabeth had talked to each other about how this quiet time made them feel warm and good inside. They even had a secret signal. While Mommy and Daddy talked, the children worked on a puzzle or drew and colored pictures. Every so often they would glance up at their Mommy and Daddy, then look at each other and smile. This was their secret signal, saying to each other, "This is what we love the very best."

Some days Daddy didn't leave in the morning. Michael and Elizabeth knew that meant they would have a special adventure with Daddy. Once, they found a baby bird with a broken wing in the meadow. They brought it home. Daddy made a tiny splint and Mommy fed it with an eyedropper. Michael and Elizabeth nursed it until one day it was well, so they opened the door and let it fly away. Everyone was sad to see it go, but they knew it was happier living in the woods with the other birds.

Bit by bit, things started to change. Elizabeth and Michael began to have funny feelings. They didn't mention them to each other until, one day, each noticed the other one was looking sad. They grabbed each other's hand and together went to find Mommy.

"Just make sure you wear your mittens and warm sweaters. It's getting colder now," she told them.

Mommy was busy, like always, but she seemed different. Usually, she would give them a big hug and smile as she saw them off. Something was different.

All bundled up, Michael and Elizabeth went to one of their favorite places in the forest and sat on a big rock by the brook.

At first they just sat watching the fish slither by, sometimes leaping up out of the water to grab a gnat flying by, other times diving to gobble a worm wiggling along the bottom.

Then gradually they began to talk. They both had noticed changes. Things didn't feel quite the same. What was it? What was the matter? What could they do about it? Were they doing something wrong? It was scary. It made Elizabeth's tummy ache.

"Maybe we can help Mommy more," Michael said. "Maybe that will make it the way it was."

"I know!" said Elizabeth. "Let's start by getting Mommy and Daddy a surprise."

The children jumped up and began collecting forest treasures—a plump mound of moss; a rainbow of leaves, red, golden, yellow, brown, and orange; a cluster of meadow flowers of all different sizes and colors; twigs and small branches; and finally three bright blue and black feathers from a molting blue jay. Delighted with their prizes, they ran giggling home.

Suddenly, they stopped in the front yard.

"That's funny," Michael whispered. "The front door is never open."

Their treasures forgotten, holding each other close, they tiptoed into the living room.

Mommy was sitting in her favorite chair with her face in her hands. Is Mommy sick? What's the matter? Daddy was standing in front of Mommy looking sad and angry at the same time. Why is Daddy home so soon? What's the matter?

At the same moment, Mommy and Daddy turned and saw the children. Mommy jumped up and rubbed her hands across her eyes. Now, Daddy looked worried and sad instead of sad and angry. They both reached out to the children. Michael and Elizabeth rushed into their arms. They hugged and snuggled together.

"Ssh, ssh," Mommy said in her gentle voice, "it's OK, it's OK."

"There, there," Daddy said in his deep voice, "don't cry. We love you."

Exercises

1. While reading the story to your child, observe your child's reactions and body language. What was his or her expression during the *happy* part of the story? during the second half?
2. Ask your child what was his or her favorite part, and why.
3. Pick out parts from the first half of the story and ask your child how each part made him or her feel.
4. Ask your child to add things to this part of the story that would make Michael and Elizabeth feel warm and good inside.
5. Pick out parts from the second half of the story, and ask your child how each part made him or her feel.
6. Ask your child what he or she thinks Michael and Elizabeth felt about the changes in their household.
7. Ask your child if he or she thinks Michael and Elizabeth were afraid, and what they might have been afraid of.
8. Ask your child how he or she felt when Mommy, Daddy, Elizabeth, and Michael were all hugging at the end of the story.
9. Ask your child if Elizabeth and Michael should have asked their parents any questions. What might those questions be?
10. Use your child's responses to the Michael and Elizabeth story to determine what's happening in your son's or daughter's mind—what the fears are, what makes him or her feel comfortable, uncomfortable, or afraid.

11. Think of ways and honest, loving words to help him or her feel secure.
12. Ask your child to answer Michael's and Elizabeth's questions from #9.
13. If the child doesn't want to answer the questions about the Michael and Elizabeth story, don't push him or her. Come back to the story later and approach it again. If your child still resists, use one of the following exercises.

Additional Exercises to Use, When Appropriate for the Age of the Child

1. Have your child make up a story about a family. After the story is finished, ask the child how it makes him or her feel—the good feelings, the bad feelings, and, if appropriate, what makes him or her afraid.
2. Make up a story together with your child, and do the same follow-up as in #1.
3. Ask your child to draw a picture, and then ask him or her to explain to you each of the things in the picture. Use the descriptions to see how your child is feeling, and help him or her with those feelings.
4. Draw a picture together with your child, and ask your child to describe all the things in the picture. Use the descriptions to see how your child is feeling, and help him or her with those feelings.
5. Use displacement communication (as demonstrated in the samples below) to help the child cope with fears and distress.

Samples

1. State an upsetting behavior: "Sometimes four-year-old kids wet their beds."

2. State how the behavior makes the child feel: "They don't like wetting their beds. It makes them feel bad."
3. State what the child is afraid of: "Sometimes kids are afraid because they don't know what's happening when their parents aren't together anymore. And they're afraid their parents don't love them."
4. Then correct the child's frightening fantasy: "Their parents love them and will always love them, no matter what. When kids are sad or afraid, they can always talk to their parents, and they can always get hugs and kisses."

You can also use dolls, stuffed animals, and other toys with the child to encourage him or her to act out situations or feelings.

Your Child's World

Your child's environment determines his or her feelings of security and sense of self. The Michael and Elizabeth story illustrates how young children are emotionally dependent on their external world. It makes them feel either good or bad. Their systems are simple and direct.

Young children's behaviors and expressions are quick and surprisingly accurate indicators of what's going on around them. Loud, angry voices will make an infant cry, refuse food, become agitated, have trouble sleeping. A tense or angry household will cause toddlers or preschoolers to have unwarranted temper tantrums; withdraw into themselves; revert to bed-wetting; show increased thumb sucking or nail chewing; have poor appetites, trouble sleeping, or nightmares; and exhibit uncharacteristic agitation and aggressiveness, or their opposites, lethargy and indifference.

If the disturbing incident in the environment is of short duration, the child's behavior will return to what is normal for him or her almost immediately; this is a phenomenon specific to this age group, 0–5. If the negative atmosphere is ongoing—coldness between the adults; indifference, impatience, or irritation toward the child; or a general lack of warmth, caring, and support—the child will mirror this behavior, as well as exhibit the behaviors mentioned earlier. These behaviors will become ingrained and will be the child's predictable response both within the household and outside when interacting with others.

Children of this age act and react instinctively. They do not have layers of experience or memories to reinforce the negative response, unless the experience becomes continuous. Children naturally are energetic, seek to please, and take things happily at face value. Their needs are simple: food, shelter, clothing, and love.

Children's self-image begins with their early experiences in their household. If the home is loving, cheerful, and supportive, then they themselves will feel lovable, cheery, and supported. They will exhibit this same behavior toward both themselves and others. The opposite is also true.

Small children act out their feelings about themselves and those around them when they play with toys. When Maria picks up her doll or stuffed animal, cradles it in her arms, coos, and kisses it, she is showing how she feels about herself and how she is being treated. When she fusses, "No! No! No!" and spanks the doll or flings it on the floor, she could well be acting out what she has been taught is correct behavior and how she feels about herself. Similarly, the way little Johnny treats his toys or stuffed animals is, again, an indication of how he sees himself in his world.

Developmental Issues

1. **Egocentricity:** The child views the world as being there to support him; when his needs are met, the child is happy; when his needs are interrupted, the child is fearful and angry.

    - The child feels responsible for changes that occur. He or she will feel that it's his or her fault when something "bad" happens.

2. **Cognitive development:** Cognitive development is limited. The child responds emotionally to what is happening around him or her.
3. **Trust:** Does the world feel safe and providing? "How good and lovable am I?"
4. **Autonomy:** "Is there a separation between me and the world?"
   - The child is beginning to separate from the mother and needs the father as an ally to help him separate.
5. **Initiative:** "When I gurgle, Mother comes."
6. **Social development:** Playtime with family members and other children plays an important role in social development:
   - Identification with same-sex parent.
   - Conflict: independence and self-assurance versus pleasure in and need for closeness.
   - The child physically acts out feelings and needs.

Divorce and the Child

A divorce causes substantial changes in a child's world. The infant or very young child operates primarily on the emotional and physical levels. He or she isn't worried about what friends are going to think or how to pay for college tuition. These may be concerns of the parent but not of the child. Children of this age operate strictly on the most basic and immediate levels.

Children's specific and basic needs are:

- A full tummy
- A warm bed
- A dry, clean body and clothes
- Hugs and kisses

When these needs are met, it doesn't matter whether they occur in a new place or whether it's Daddy, Mommy, or a surrogate caretaker who is performing the task.

The parent or surrogate is the source of the child's contentment. Meeting these basic needs for the child is a simple assignment. The challenge to parents during a divorce is to protect the child from the parent's fears, anxiety, and confusion. When the child feels the parent's anxiety, the child, in turn, will become anxious and fearful. Even if the physical needs are being met, the infant, toddler, or preschooler will feel emotionally insecure and afraid in his or her world, likely with long-term consequences. This is building block time—insecurity set at this stage is *very* difficult to reverse later.

Family Disruption Issues

1. Developmental issues can be threatened or strengthened by a breakup between the mother and father. Some children will become more mature, some less so.
2. The child's fears about love and security mean that reassurance of love, a familiar routine, consistency, the meeting of physical needs, and parental emotional stability are all vital during the time of transition, as they were before and will continue to be during the child's life.
3. Changes in or interruption of love and physical needs causes fear and anger.

Some Don'ts and Do's

- Don't argue within your child's hearing.
- Don't have angry discussions about your husband or wife with a third party when the child is present.
- Don't have emotional telephone conversations within the child's hearing.

- Don't rant and rave out loud within the child's hearing.
- Do make sure the child spends time with each parent as much as possible.
- Do tell the child the divorce is not his or her fault.
- Do carry out your normal routine as much as possible.
- Do keep the child's schedule as predictable as possible.
- Do take time out for hugs, kisses, and cuddling.
- Do remember to say, "I love you."

The Age of the Child Does Make a Difference

The younger the child is, the more in tune he or she will be to your feelings and moods. If you smile, he or she will smile in return. The older preschool child will ask questions when he or she is ready or when he or she doesn't understand what's going on. Answer the questions simply and honestly. If something unpleasant does happen, explain the situation reasonably—not emotionally—to the child. Afterward, distract the child with an activity he or she enjoys, to take his or her mind off of it and provide something pleasant to think about.

Suggested Activities

- A bubble bath with favorite bath toys
- A favorite story
- A favorite game
- A walk
- Any activity that you and the child enjoy sharing

These activities will have the added benefit of distracting you as well!

Divorce and the aftermath are a very hard time. This experience does not have to be destructive to infants or young children if they know they are loved, cared for, and protected. When food is in their tummy, "blankie" is on their bed, and their favorite red boots are in their closet, they will be all right and will reward you daily with their joy.

Always remember to say, "I love you."

Your Child's Emotional Signals, and Your Appropriate Responses

Facial Expressions

- Frowning
- Sad
- Angry

Your Response

- Your caring attention usually will be all that's necessary:
  - — Pick up your child and hug, kiss, rock, or just hold him or her.
  - — If there's time, sit and read to the child, play toys with him or her, or distract the child with some shared activity.
- Observe your own behavior and see if it could be triggering your child's. If it is, use this signal from your child to help you work on your own feelings.
- If the child is old enough, ask him or her why he or she is sad or angry.
  - — Talk it through with him or her.

— If the child is too young for a dialogue, cuddle and talk lovingly to the child.

Body Language

- Withdrawn
- Huddled
- Turning away
- Closed
- Repetitive motion (banging an object, constant rocking)

Your Response

- Often, caring attention is all that is needed, or an invitation to join you in an activity.
- Frequently give your child hugs, kisses, and just plain old-fashioned holding.
- Again, observe your own body language and behavior.
- If the age of the child permits, ask what's the matter.
- For younger children, hold them and talk to them. Your child is very responsive to the playful or loving tone of your voice.

Possible Feelings

- Fear, anxiety, nervousness, timidity, anger, sadness

Possible Behaviors

- Reverting to younger behaviors in the areas of toilet training, motor skills, language, eating habits, sleeping habits, returning to the bottle, crawling instead of walking, returning to more primitive communication, having toilet "accidents"

- Acting out anger or anxiety: crying, tantrums, aggressive behavior toward inanimate objects or toward peers, adults, or self; having new fears: the dark, heights, animals, and the like; clinging, fretting, teeth grinding (usually this age is too young for this behavior), nail biting, stuttering, and other nervous habits; putting self down; changes in social activity; refusing food, exhibiting a poor appetite or an excessively increased appetite; resisting going to sleep, trouble sleeping, frequent waking, nightmares; showing less initiative, acting more passive or lethargic; and so forth

Interpretation of Facial Expressions, Body Language, and Behaviors

- Changes in your child's facial expressions, body language, or behavior that last more than a few days indicate distress and fear.
- Fear is caused by a break in or loss of physical or emotional needs being unsatisfied.
- Anger is a reflection of the anger of one or both parents, or arises because the child feels out of control of his or her environment or because he or she is angry at the change in his or her environment.
- Unusual timidity or nervousness indicates fear and anxiety about what's happening in the child's world.

Your Response

- Don't panic. All of these behaviors help you stay in touch with your child's state of mind and are the child's natural response to, and means of coping with, his or her world.
- Be sure not to let your child's behavior make you feel or act anxious. That will only add to his or her feelings of insecurity and will heighten the responses exhibited already.

What to Do

- Ages 0–5
  - — Reassure your child that he is loved and his life is secure.
  - — Give physical affection frequently: holding, hugging, kissing, rocking.
  - — Maintain as normal a routine as possible.
  - — Avoid making loud or sudden noises.
  - — Avoid parental warfare.
  - — Share pleasurable activities with your child.
- Ages 3–5
  - — Discuss in simple terms the divorce and what will change. If your child's eyes glaze over or he or she begins to fidget, stop the discussion for the time being.
  - — Be ready to answer your child's questions as they come up.
  - — Express your love for your child, and tell him or her that the divorce is not his or her fault.

If you find you need additional methods of dealing with these behaviors, contact your pediatrician. Doctors have seen it all.

Whether your child's behavior is caused by the atmosphere around him or her as a result of the divorce or is simply a predictable level of anxiety normal for a young child growing up, the child will survive and thrive in your loving care.

Summary

- The early childhood environment that fulfills the basic physical and emotional needs of the child is a guarantee of his or her future self-esteem and self-worth.
- Your child's feelings of security are built on the satisfaction of basic physical and emotional needs:
  - — A full tummy
  - — A warm bed
  - — A dry, clean body and clothes
  - — Lots of hugs and kisses
  - — Love
- Some behaviors are normal developmental behaviors and aren't the result of the divorce or the breakup of the family.
- Your child is an immediate and accurate echo of his or her environment.
- A divorce does not rob you of your good parenting skills.
- Use your own best parental instincts and good common sense to meet your child's needs for love and physical well-being and you will ensure that your child gets off to a happy, well-adjusted start in his or her life.

Chapter 2
Early Childhood
(AGES 6–9)

"Star Light, Star Bright"

Instructions

For children who are 6 or 7, a parent may need to read the following story to the child, or read along with him or her. At the end of each section of the story, the parent may need to help the child with the questions and exercises.

Children who are 8 or 9 will likely be able to read the story easily, with a little help from a parent. The child may want to share the exercises and questions with a parent, or do them alone.

For all children 6–9, the parents and children can enjoy doing the exercises and questions together. The child can also do them alone. The exercises and questions can be used over and over. How he or she answers the questions or does the exercises can change as time goes by.

Tell your child, "This story is written just for you. It is a story about the Apple family and what happens when Mr. Apple and Mrs. Apple decide to get divorced. At the end of each part of the story, there are questions and exercises for you. If you have trouble with a word, ask me or your [Mom/Dad], sister, or brother to help you."

The Apple Family Story

The Apple family lived in Appleton. Apples were everywhere in Appleton. Apple trees, apple umbrellas, apple tables, even the Apple Family Store shaped just like a B-I-G apple. The Apple Family Store sold a lot of apple things—crunchy apples, apple juice, apple cider, candied apples, apple cake, apple pie, apple ice cream, plus many, many other apple things. Mr. and Mrs. Apple loved their Apple Store. Mom Apple had round rosy cheeks that looked just like—well, apples! When she smiled they looked even more like apples, and she smiled a lot.

The three Apple children were McIntosh, or Mac for short, who was 9 years old; Delicious, Delly for short, who was 8 years old; and Pippin, Pip for short, who was 6. Each child had favorite things in the store. Mac loved the apple baseball bats. He could hardly wait for his tenth birthday to join Little League with his own apple bat. His other favorite thing was the *Apple Book of Names.* It listed the name of every apple grown in the world. He liked to look up *McIntosh* in it. Delly had two special favorites in the store. First, she liked the apple aprons. Second, she liked the apple bubble bath. One day she said she wanted an apple bat just like Mac's, because she liked to play softball, too. Pippin loved the wind-up apple toys that scooted all over the floor and counters. His very favorite things in the store were all the bushels and bushels of apples in many colors and sizes. And, of course, he wanted an apple bat, too.

After school, each child had a special job in the Apple Store. Mac, because he was the biggest and strongest, helped Dad Apple unload the apple trucks and refill all the bushel baskets with the right apples. Delly put on her own apple apron and helped Mom Apple bake the apple tarts, apple pies, apple cookies, and apple cakes. Yum! Pip had fun winding up the apple toys and sending them racing over the counters and floor. But his favorite job was to get a clean, white cloth and polish the apples in the brimming baskets.

Questions and Exercises

1. Who did you like best in the Apple family?
2. What was your favorite thing in the Apple Store?
3. Which job did you like the best?
4. If you had a store, what kind would it be? What special things would you sell in it?
5. Draw a picture of the Apple family.
6. Draw a picture of your family.
7. Draw a big apple and several stems. Color and cut out the apple and the stems. Tack the apple up on the wall. When friends come over, see who can stick the stem closest to the top of the apple blindfolded.
8. Draw three apples, and color one like a McIntosh, one like a Golden Delicious, and one like a Pippin.
9. Draw an apple that looks like a dog.
10. Draw a house with apple shapes.

Springtime in Appleton

It was springtime in Appleton. One of Mac, Delly, and Pip's favorite things to do when the weather was warm was to go outside after dinner and make wishes on the first star. Pip had just learned the poem "Star Light, Star Bright" all the way through. As the weather grew warmer, the apple blossoms began to burst into bloom. The children loved the sweet smell of the beautiful white flowers.

One afternoon, Delly walked into the kitchen. Mom Apple was stirring a big pot of chicken soup. Delly smelled the onions and sage and all the good things Mom put in the broth. Mom turned around to move the pot off the stove. Her eyes were all red. Delly thought she looked like she had been crying.

"Mom, is something wrong?" she asked.

"No, Darling. Maybe the onions got in my eyes. Come help me set the table," Mom said. "We are having our first apple crisp this spring."

After that, things seemed different. Mac, Delly, and Pip noticed Mom wasn't laughing as much as usual, and Dad frowned when he thought no one was looking. Mac began to feel uncomfortable. Delly woke up with stomach aches. Sometimes, Pip crawled into bed with Delly, saying he was having nightmares. Even the Apple Store seemed quiet. Something was not right.

At dinner one night, Dad Apple cleared his throat and said, "Mac, Delly, Pip, something very important is going to happen. It will change our family, and we will have to help each other. Your Mom and I are going to get a divorce."

Mac, Delly, and Pip spoke at once: "What?" "Oh! Why?" "What will happen to us?" "What will happen to the Apple Store?" Pip burst into tears.

Mom spoke gently, saying, "I know this is very sudden. It's scary. Come, Pip, sit on my lap. Once we talk about it, it won't be as frightening. Let's answer as many questions as we can. First of all, Mom and Dad love you very much and always will."

Mac asked, "Will we still live in this house?"

Dad said, "Yes. Later that may change. For now you will live here as you always have."

Pip asked, "Is it something I did?"

"Oh, no," said Mom, "don't think that. It's a change between Dad and me. It's nothing any of you did."

Dad added, "I'm going to live in the yellow house down the street next to the Apple Store. Mac, Delly, and Pip, we'll set it up so that you can come stay with me part of the time."

Delly asked, "What will happen to the Apple Store? Will we go to the same school?"

Dad answered, "We'll still have the Apple Store. You'll come by after school as you always have. Your school won't change."

Mom said, "Most things will be just the same. As changes happen, we will all sit down together and talk about them."

Dad said, "We are still a family, and your Mom and I love you very, very much."

Mom and Dad Apple hugged and kissed Mac, Delly, and Pip as they always did before the children went up to bed.

The children felt better. Now they knew what was going on. They were not happy that Mom and Dad were not going to live together anymore and that some things were going to be different. But most things were going to be the same—and they knew Mom and Dad loved them.

Questions

1. How did this part of the story make you feel?
2. How is your family like the Apple family?
3. How is your family not like the Apple family?
4. When your Mom and Dad told you about the divorce, how did you feel? Do you still have those feelings?
5. Have you talked to your Mom, Dad, sister, brother, or someone about your feelings? Feelings are the hardest things to talk about, especially feelings that make you feel bad. Talking about them can make you feel better.

6. Do you live with your Mom or Dad?
7. Do you see your other parent as much as you would like?
8. Can you talk to your other parent on the phone?
9. Who is your favorite person to talk to?
10. What are some of the changes that have happened now that your Mom and Dad don't live together?
11. Is your house the same? Is your school the same? Do you see the same friends?
12. Are there some questions you would like to ask about the divorce? Who can you ask these questions?

Summer in Appleton

Summer in Appleton was the most beautiful time of the year. This summer was very busy for Mac, Delly, and Pip. They helped Dad Apple fix his new house. Sometimes they all stayed overnight with Dad Apple. When Mac or Delly or Pip had something special to do, the other two children would stop by for dinner with Dad Apple and spend the night. Mac went to baseball practice every afternoon. Sometimes, Mom Apple took Mac to practice. Sometimes, Dad Apple left the Apple Store early to pick Mac up. Sometimes, Mom and Dad went to the games together. Pip found a special apple tree at Dad's house. The branches were low, and Pip could pick the apples and watch the branches spring back up. Delly finally got her own apple bat, and Mac helped her practice hitting.

One day, Pip, Delly, and Mac were sorting their clothes and toys. Each one made three stacks. One stack was to stay at Mom's house. One stack was to go to Dad's house. And one was to take to school for the toy and clothes sale. Delly put her blue sweater on the sale stack. She said, "I don't like this sweater. It makes me feel sad."

Mac said, "It used to be your favorite."

"I know," said Delly, "but I was wearing it when Mom and Dad told us about the divorce."

Pip said, "I miss all of us living together like we used to. Maybe Mom and Dad will get together again. Do you think they will?" Both Mac and Delly shook their heads.

"I don't know," said Delly, "but I don't think so. They both seem happier now."

"Sometimes," said Mac, "I feel angry that it happened."

Both Pip and Delly nodded their heads. "I do, too," they said together. They all felt better, knowing that they were not the only one feeling angry. They were happy they could tell each other how they felt.

Mac said, "We're lucky. We know Mom and Dad love us. We can still be with them. We're still a family even if we don't live in the same house."

"Not many things have changed," said Delly. "And I'm glad Dad lives so close. If I forget something, I don't have far to go."

"Yeah," said Pip. "Now I have more room for my stuff."

Mac said, "I'm glad we can tell each other if we feel sad or angry. Then we don't have to feel lonely."

"I feel that way, too," said Delly. "And the most important thing is that Mom and Dad love us very much. We're together and we can help each other."

It took Mac, Delly, and Pip several trips to carry all their stacks downstairs. Dad Apple drove up just as they finished. They loaded the clothes and toys into the car to take them to school for the sale. Mom Apple waved from the doorway as they drove off.

Questions and Exercises

1. Do you feel you are different because your Mom and Dad are divorced?

2. How do you feel different?
3. Do you think about your Mom and Dad getting back together again? Usually, when people get divorced, they don't get back together.
4. Do you feel you did something to make the divorce happen? Do you feel you could have done something to make it not happen?

   Often, children have these feelings, but it is important to know that a divorce is a change between the husband and wife and that the children did not cause the divorce to happen.

5. Do you have some of the feelings the Apple children talked about? What feelings do you have?
6. Everyone feels angry, sad, or lonely at times. Who is someone you can talk to when you have these feelings?
7. What are some of the things in your life that have changed since the divorce?
8. What are some changes you like?
9. What are some good things that have stayed the same?
10. It's all right not to feel good about something that happens that you don't like. The next step is to accept it, if it has to be that way, and make the best of it. One way to do that is to do something you enjoy doing that does make you feel good.
11. Make a list of things you like to do, and try to do at least one of them every day.

Summary

1. Your Mom and Dad love you very much.
2. It is your parents' divorce. You did not cause it, but it will cause changes to happen in your life.
3. You won't like all the changes, but you can make the best of them.
4. It's very important to have someone to talk to, to help you feel better when you have questions or are upset.
5. Make a list of your favorite things to do, and choose one to do each day.

Chapter 3
Preadolescence
(AGES 10–12)

"Knock, Knock!" "Who's There?"

Instructions

This chapter is written especially for children like you who are 10 to 12 years old with parents going through a divorce.

The chapter begins with jokes to help you take your mind off things that are bothering you. You may find one you really like, or you may think of a joke you know already. You can even make up your own joke. Jokes are very useful. When something happens that hurts you or makes you angry or afraid, you can think of one of these silly jokes or one of your own favorite ones and feel better.

The rest of the chapter is made up of stories about people your age who are dealing with the same things you are. It helps to know that you're not the only one with feelings like yours or with parents who are getting a divorce. Some of these stories will feel familiar and will help you understand your own feelings and situation better.

After each story, there are questions and exercises for you to do. Your answers are important information for you to use to help you with your feelings and your parents' divorce. Use a separate sheet of paper for your answers.

Sometimes it's easy to talk to one of your parents or someone you feel close to about your feelings and what's happening. You may want to share this chapter with them. If it isn't easy for you to talk about your feelings with someone else, then you may want to read and work on this chapter by yourself. You choose what works best for you.

Jokes and Riddles

"Knock, knock!"
"Who's there?"
"Fido."
"Fido who?"
"Fido want to, I don't have to!"

Question: "What did the mayonnaise say to the refrigerator?"
Answer: "Hey, close the door! I'm dressing!"

Question: "Why did the chicken cross the road?"
Answer: "Because it was his turn to play Tic Tac Toe!"

Question: "Why do mother kangaroos hate rainy days?"
Answer: "Because the children have to play inside."

Question: "What bus crossed the ocean?"
Answer: "Colum-bus."

Question: "What pool can't you swim in?"
Answer: "A car-pool."

Question: "When do clocks die?"
Answer: "When their time is up."

Question: "What stars go to jail?"
Answer: "Shooting stars."

Questions and Exercises

- Write down some of your favorite jokes and riddles.
- What are your favorite things to do at home? at school?
- Who is your best friend?
- What is your favorite movie? TV show? rock group?
- What things worry you the most?
- What do you not like about yourself?
- What do you like most about yourself?

Moving to a New Town

Barbara's family has just moved to a new town. It's her first day of school in the sixth grade. Her mother drops her off at school and gives her a big hug. Barbara has butterflies in her stomach. Everything is so new!

"At least," Barbara thinks, "we've gotten used to the new house, and I've made friends with Sara, who lives next door and is in my class, too."

As she walks down the long, unfamiliar hallway to her classroom, she thinks to herself, "Oh, I hope Sara speaks to me."

She opens the classroom door slowly, and there in front of her is a sea of new faces.

"Oh, no! Am I late? Am I in the wrong room? Where's Sara? I wish I could drop in a hole! Is this skirt too childish? Too grown-up?"

Just then, the teacher ("She has nice eyes") walks up to Barbara.

"Barbara," she says with a warm smile, "we're so glad you're a part of our class. You'll have to tell us about your old school and what you were learning in your classes there."

She leads Barbara over to the empty desk next to...Sara! Then the teacher turns to Barbara and says, "We sit alphabetically the first week. I think you already know Sara Miller."

That night at dinner, Barbara and her brother tell their mother and father all about their new school.

"Mom," Barbara says, "thanks for taking me to school today. Sara says the bus stop is near here. Tomorrow, she's going to show me where it is. She says there are lots of kids from our class that live around here. Isn't that great? You won't have to drive."

Later in the conversation, Barbara volunteers, "Anne, who sits right behind me in class, said she really liked my skirt and wanted to know where I got it."

As Barbara goes to sleep that night she thinks, "Well, for a new grade in a new school, not bad—not bad at all. I think it's going to be all right."

Questions

- Have you ever moved to new town? to a new house?
- How did you feel?
- What did you worry about most?
- Have you ever changed schools?
- How did you feel?
- What did you worry about most the first day?

Whether you have or haven't moved or changed schools, think of a new situation you've been in and answer the following:

- What was the first thing that happened that made you feel welcome or good?
- What were you good at that helped you fit in? Was it sports? schoolwork? something else?

- Was there a group you were a part of?
- What made it hard for you to feel you belonged?
- What or who made it easy?
- How do you feel about the opposite sex?
- How do they treat you?
- Do you have friends of the opposite sex?
- In what ways do you feel more grown-up this year than last?

Eric's Favorite Mug

One day Eric comes home after school to find his mother packing dishes in the kitchen. It's been two months since his father moved out of their apartment, and two weeks after that his father had called Eric's mother to say he wanted a divorce.

Eric was really upset when his father left. He was even more upset when the divorce announcement happened. He began to feel he didn't know what to expect from one day to the next. Everything felt uncertain. And now something else was changing.

"Mom, why are you packing the dishes? What's going on?"

His mother turns to him and says, "For now, it looks like we'll be able to stay here, but your father and I decided to try to make the changes that are bound to come as gradual as possible, instead of all at one time. So, I'm dividing up some of the things so that when the final decisions are made and we have to split things up, it won't seem so sudden."

"Well, it all seems sudden to me, but no one's asking me," Eric mutters. "I wish I knew what was going on around here. Who knows what's going to happen next that I don't know about?"

"I know this isn't easy for you children," his mother says. "It isn't easy for any of us, but the only thing we can do is accept that this is how it's going to be and try to help each other make it as smooth as possible."

Getting angry, Eric answers, "Who would have thought when I was 10 that two years later everything was going to blow up in my face? You and Dad decide to change everything, and Ellen, Jack, and I are just thrown into the middle of it." His voice rises. "Who knows, maybe in two more years the whole world will blow up!"

He starts to stomp out of the room. His mother calls him back, saying, "Eric, come back here. That's just what I meant. We can all get unhappy and angry and only make this time even worse for ourselves and everybody else—or we can decide to learn how to make the best of it, feel good about ourselves, and make the whole thing a lot easier for all of us. I could really use your help with this mess. Which of these mugs is your favorite?"

Questions

- How did you first learn that your parents were getting a divorce?
- What did you feel?
- Had one of your parents moved out of your home?
- When did one of your parents move out?
- How did you feel about all these changes?
- Do you want to talk to someone about your feelings? Is there someone?
- What worries you the most about what has happened?
- What are you worried will happen?
- Can you ask someone about these things so that you'll feel better about your worries?

- When you get upset, what do you do? Does that help you feel better? Are there better ways?
- Since the time your parents started getting divorced, how have you gotten used to the changes?
- How have you learned to make the best of it?

Dad Moves to Colorado

Steve's parents have been getting a divorce for two years. When it began, his mother and father didn't talk to each other very much.

Steve and his younger brother, John, live with their mother and visit their father just about every weekend. Sometimes their father comes by during the week and takes them out for dinner.

Recently, Steve's mother has been talking to his father on the phone more and more. She ends up getting very angry. The conversations that upset her the most seem to be about who the boys will live with after the divorce. When Steve and John visit their father, the same subject comes up. Both parents question the boys about what the other parent is saying, which just makes matters worse. Steve and John can hear the anger in their parents' voices when they talk about each other. The subject of where the boys will live has become more important, because their father has decided to move to another town. This change will make visits during the week impossible and the weekend visits much harder than before.

The fighting between his parents upsets Steve very much. He doesn't know what he can do to help. When he's with one of them, he feels disloyal to the other. He feels caught in the middle all the time. With his father planning to move away, Steve is more upset than ever. His father has always been there when he's needed him.

"I guess I can call him on the phone, but it's not the same. Dad's always been around to talk to about all the stuff that's happening at school. Even when I don't exactly tell him, he seems to know what I'm dealing with, growing up. I just feel better when he's nearby. Mom's great but she doesn't know about being a boy. I love them both, but their fighting and sticking me in the middle makes me mad—and I'm really angry at Dad for moving away. I guess Dad's right, though. This is how things are, and the sooner I accept that, the better I'm going to feel. It won't be all bad visiting Dad in Colorado, either!"

Questions

- Did your parents quarrel a lot before and during their divorce?
- Do they still quarrel?
- What did or do they quarrel about?
- How does the quarreling make you feel?
- Do your parents ask you about the other parent?
- Do you feel you have to side with one or the other parent?
- Do you feel caught in the middle?
- Do you sometimes get angry at one or both of your parents about this?
- Which parent do you live with?
- Is your other parent nearby? Do you see or talk to that parent as much as you'd like?
- Do you think you can take care of what's bothering you and deal with the situation?
- Can you talk to your parents about what's bothering you?
- Is there someone else you can talk to?

Lisa's Two Homes

Lisa's parents got a divorce when she was 10. She is now 11. She spends two weeks a month with her father and two weeks with her mother. At first, whatever she needed seemed to be where she wasn't. It drove her crazy until she figured out how to make it work. Her parents live close enough that she can go to the same school, and some of her friends live near her father's place and some near her mother's. All in all, Lisa feels things are working out pretty well since the divorce.

"If only Mom weren't so sad all the time. It makes me feel like it's up to me to make her happy," Lisa confides to a friend. "Like tonight, I really want to go to the movies with you but I can't leave Mom all alone. It's not that I don't have fun with her, but I need to do things with my friends, too. For now, I just don't feel right leaving her. Maybe next week, OK?"

Questions

- Do you feel you have to take care of your mother or father?
- Do you have enough time with your friends?
- Do you have friends whose parents are divorced?
- Do you talk to each other about the divorces?
- Are you doing more at home since the divorce?
- Do you spend more time with your parents and family since the divorce? Is that OK with you, or would you like to have more time for friends and other activities?
- Can you and your parents talk about it?
- Does spending time with your parents and family help you to get used to the divorce and the changes that are happening?

Talking to Mrs. Kahill

Jen's parents have been divorced for a year. Since then, she has gotten used to seeing her dad during vacations and talking to him on the phone at least once a week.

She and her mother do a lot of things together. They enjoy going shopping together and talking about movies they both like. Jen pitches in with the chores around the house more now than before the divorce. Maybe because she's 12 she is able to help more. Or maybe it's because there's no one else to do the jobs. Whatever the reasons are, it does make Jen feel good to help her mother and to know her mother thinks she's responsible.

Even though Jen feels very close to her mother, sometimes there are things she doesn't want to talk to her about.

As Jen says to herself, "I can't really talk to Mom about the divorce and some of the things that happen at school. She has enough on her mind. I don't want her to worry about me, too. I'm not sure she'd understand how much I miss Dad, or why I don't want to spend the night at Victoria's anymore, now that she wears a bra and I don't. Also, Victoria's been hanging around with Nat, and I feel left out. I don't want to spend all night hearing how great he is and how much fun they have. Most of all, I don't want to talk to Mom about Dad's girlfriend. I don't even know if she knows about Jackie. I'm sure not going to tell her! I wish I could, though. Jackie makes me feel uncomfortable. Dad acts differently when he's with her. He's always looking at her and holding her hand. I feel left out. I don't like to think about Dad with her that way. If I'd known about Jackie, I wouldn't have gone to Dad's for spring vacation. I've got to think of someone to talk to about this. It's really bothering me. Maybe tomorrow at school I'll talk to Mrs. Kahill. She really helped last fall."

Questions

- Do either of your parents have a new boyfriend or girlfriend?
- How does that make you feel?
- Do you like the new person or people? How does he or she treat you?
- Do you feel pulled between your loyalty to your other parent and liking the new person?
- Do you feel close enough to one or both of your parents to talk to them about this subject? If not, is there someone else you can talk to?

Mason Helps His Sister

Mason, who's 12, has just come home from school to find his younger sister, Iris, who's 10, sitting in the kitchen crying.

"What's the matter?" he asks.

"I'm so mad," she shrieks. "Mom's making me miss the party at school Friday because it's my weekend to visit Dad. It's not fair! They're the ones who got the divorce, but we're the ones who have to change our lives!"

"Yeah, I know," Mason agrees. "I had to miss practice, so I couldn't play in the game last week. Let's call Dad and see if you can go Saturday instead, but first we'd better tell Mom."

Just then, their mother walks into the room.

"I think that's a good idea if your father agrees," she says, "but there will be some times when visiting your father will interrupt something else that comes up. We'll have to take these one at a time. It's just as important for you to have time with your dad as it is for him. We're all new at this. Let's try to make it work as well as we can. After a while, things will settle down. Sometimes you'll have to change your plans, and sometimes your father and I will have to change ours. It's not perfect. Nothing is, but we'll make it work the best we can."

Questions

- Do you feel that the divorce and the new situation at home have affected your routine at school and with your friends?
- Do you feel caught up by the change or conflict in your family just when you want to spend more time outside your home?
- Do you feel you have to take care of a sister, brother, or parent more than you did before?
- Do you feel it's up to you to solve the problems in your home?
- Do you feel you have to put your feelings and what you want after what the family wants?
- Can you talk to your father and mother and work out a way to take turns?

Summary

The stories you just read are about the things that usually bother people your age whose parents divorce. The following is a list of what those things are. Read the list and see which ones are on your mind.

- Being worried or afraid of what's happening in your family or what will happen
- Feeling alone
- Feeling pulled between your parents

- Feeling that you love both parents, or feeling that you side with one of them
- Feeling the loss of the parent who doesn't live with you
- Feeling the divorce is your fault
- Feeling angry at one or both of your parents
- Feeling you have to take care of a parent or fill in for the other parent
- Feeling upset about your parents' dating or remarrying—is it OK to like the new person?
- Feeling that your family and your home are taking too much of your time and keeping you from something you'd rather do

List any other feelings you may be having.

The best way to deal with these feelings and your parents' divorce is to realize that sometimes families break up. It happens. It's not the end of the world. It has happened to you, but it was not your fault and you will survive.

Whatever you're feeling, others your age are feeling the same things. Your feelings aren't wrong or bad, but you need to get through them or they'll get in your way. You can either talk to your parents about what's bothering you or talk to another adult you're comfortable talking to. You can choose to keep your feelings to yourself, think about them as part of getting used to the new situation, and then let them go.

Your parents' divorce has caused changes for you, but there will be other changes that will happen in your life and feelings that will come with these changes. Some things you'll like and some you won't. Change itself isn't bad. It's how you deal with it that makes it work for you or not. You'll see, as you get used to each new situation, that the feelings will go away by themselves if you let them.

Building Self-Esteem

Questions to Help You Feel Good About Yourself

- What do I do well?
- What are my hobbies?
- Who are my best friends?
- What are some things that may change?
- What's good about these changes? What's bad?
- What things will be the same?
- What's good about them? What's bad?
- How would I like things to be?
- Which of these things do I have now? I'll concentrate on them.
- Who are some people I can talk to and be with who make me feel good? Make a list of these people.
- When I feel upset, I'll make sure to spend some time with one of the people on my list.

Part Two

Developmental Stages and Divorce for Ages 13–19

Chapter 4
Early Adolescence
(AGES 13–14)

"Don't Stop Thinking About Tomorrow"
—BY CHRISTINE MCVIE, SUNG BY FLEETWOOD MAC

Instructions

This chapter is written specifically for young people like you who are 13 or 14 years old and have parents going through a divorce. The purpose of this chapter is to help you look at the very specific ways your parents' divorce is affecting you. It will also give you the means to deal with these issues so that the divorce experience won't have a long-term effect on you. Fleetwood Mac's words say it best: If you take care of today, tomorrow "will be here better than before."

The chapter is made up of stories that cover the issues that are on your mind right now—issues that a year ago wouldn't have occurred to you and that won't matter to you a year or two from now.

The questions are included in the chapter to help you pinpoint how each issue is affecting you in your situation. Your answers will give you the information you need to handle your parents' divorce successfully. Use a separate sheet of paper for your answers.

As you read through the chapter, you will discover that others your age are concerned with the same issues you are. You will probably find that some of their experiences are familiar. It helps to know that you are not the only one.

You may want to share this chapter with your parents or talk about it with someone else whose advice you trust. You may feel you'd rather read and work on the chapter by yourself. You choose what works best for you.

Growing Up Is More like a Hurricane than a Bed of Roses

Most young people your age are a lot more aware of themselves than they were when they were 11 or 12.

They think they stand out like a "sore thumb." Everyone is watching them and will notice any mistake they make or anything about them that's different from the rest of the group. They're apt to be very critical of themselves and others, although they may appear not to care or notice.

This sudden awareness has a specific cause and purpose. It's caused by a rampaging hormone hurricane that creates sensitive feelings, sudden spurts of energy, and emotional ups and downs. The purpose of this new 20/20 vision is to alert the young person to the physical changes, mental growth, and emotional development of the "new" person he or she is becoming.

The changes can be sudden and startling. They are certainly new. Just like an animal that sheds its skin or shell to grow to a new size, the young person moves out of the protective shell of childhood. Stripped of the old, familiar skin, the young person is particularly sensitive to what's going on around him or her and how it can affect him or her.

Usually young people feel very exposed during this time and look to family and friends for security and a feeling of belonging. It's no wonder that, with all that's happening inside, any change that occurs in their surroundings can be especially hard for them to deal with.

Questions

- How did you first notice your hormone hurricane? From physical changes? emotional changes? mental changes?
- Did you discuss them with a friend? with one of your parents?
- What do you like about the changes in yourself?
- What don't you like?
- What do you do to make these changes easier for you to deal with?

The Spring Dance

A group of young people 13 and 14 years old have gotten together after school to plan the spring dance. Most of the decisions have been made, and the meeting is beginning to break up.

"Hey, I just noticed Jessica wasn't here," says Rob. "Anybody know what happened to her?"

"You're right," Catherine says. "I hadn't noticed she was missing, and she was the one who volunteered to have the post-dance party. Come to think of it, I didn't see her at school today, either."

"The only thing I know," Melissa volunteers, "is what I overheard Jackie saying at school. Something about a big fight between Jessica's parents."

"Oh, no," says Catherine, "not that again. She's really had a hard time all year because of them. Every time there's a fight, one of them takes off. The other one goes into the bedroom, slams the door, and won't come out, and Jessica is stuck taking care of the children. I don't know how she stands it. It would be better if her parents just got a divorce!"

"I don't know," says Tom. "I've been through one and it's not a lot of fun, I can tell you."

"Yeah, well," Rob breaks in, "my parents have been divorced for three years now. It sure was awful at the beginning but everything's pretty much settled down now, and I've gotten used to two families and all that. I think anything's better than the way it was before: shouting and fighting one minute and cold silence the next, Mom telling me how bad Dad is, and Dad complaining about Mom."

"Hey, I'm beginning to feel left out," says Susan. "Am I the only kid in the world whose parents aren't divorced?"

"That's right," says Rob grinning. "It's not normal to be normal." Everyone laughs.

Then Catherine says, "I'll give Jessica a call when I get home and let her off the hook for the post-dance party. Who knows what'll be going on for her by then? Maybe it'll give her a chance to talk about it. Poor kid."

"Well," Rob says, "now what are we going to do about the post-dance party? I guess we'd better stay a little longer and figure that out."

Questions

- Before your parents decided to get a divorce, did you notice them fighting? arguing? treating each other badly? giving each other the cold, silent treatment? engaging in other negative behavior? List those behaviors.
- How did their behavior make you feel?
- During the divorce, how have your parents been acting toward each other?
- Do you get caught in the middle between them?

- Do you side with one or the other parent? If you do side with one parent, what are the reasons?
- Do either or both of your parents turn to you to let off steam? to complain about the other parent?
- Do you feel it's up to you to make things all right?
- How do the divorce and your parents' behavior affect you? make you feel?
- What would you like to see happen?
- Do you have friends whose parents are divorced?
- Can you talk to them about what's happening in your family?

The Phone Call

Jessica is fixing dinner when the phone rings. She hopes it's her father and that he and her mother will make up so that things can get back to normal. "Whatever that is," she thinks, "and for however long that lasts."

"Hello. Oh, it's you, Catherine," says Jessica.

"Hey, what a reception," says Catherine with a laugh. "Expecting a call?"

"No, not really," answers Jessica. "What happened at the meeting today? I'm sorry I missed it. I've been tied up here all day, you know, taking care of things."

"Yeah, I know. That's why I called," Catherine says. "I mean, yes, I heard about last night and, yes, I figured you'd want to know what happened at the meeting. Before I get into that, I just wanted to let you know we all thought it might be easier on you if you didn't have to worry about the post-dance party. It's up to you, but we'll understand if you want someone else to have it."

There is a pause and then with a sigh Jessica says, "I guess everyone knows about Mom and Dad. What a bitch. Oh, well.

Actually, I was really looking forward to having the party, but it's probably best if someone else does it. Things are so mixed up here. Mom stayed home from work today, but she was out of it. I just couldn't leave the twins at day care. After all the stuff last night, they kept waking up all night long, crying. I'm sure glad I didn't have any tests today."

"Oh, that reminds me," says Catherine. "The grade rankings came out today. You knocked them cold! You and Rob are still tied for first."

Then Catherine and Jessica discuss the spring dance meeting and as they are finishing up, Jessica says, "Catherine, it really helps to be able to talk to you about my parents. I think I'd blow up if I couldn't talk to someone. I don't know why it seems so much harder to put up with this year than last. I have enough trouble trying to figure myself out from day to day. When this stuff happens, I don't know whether I'm coming or going. Believe it or not, doing homework is a relief. I just wish they'd decide once and for all what they want to do with each other. Anything's got to be better than not knowing what to expect from one day to the next. I'm beginning to sound old beyond my years."

Catherine says, "Jessica, you sure seem to be managing it all fine to me. I wish I had your grades. Next time, call me and I'll come over and take care of the twins. Just kidding."

Both girls laugh and Jessica says, "See you tomorrow, and thanks for calling."

Questions

- When your parents decided to get a divorce, what upset you the most?
- Do you have friends to talk to about it?
- Did it bother you for your friends to find out that your parents were getting a divorce?

- Does what's going on at home interfere with school? with your activities? with your friends?
- In what ways? How do you feel?
- Do you have to pitch in with your brothers and sisters when one of your parents is having a hard time?
- How does that make you feel?
- How do the changes and confusion at home make you feel about you and what you're trying to do?
- Which of your parents' problems affect you? How do you handle them?
- Can you separate what are really only your parents' problems from what you have to deal with? List those.
- What's the hardest thing you've had to deal with about your parents' divorce?
- How do you handle it?

On the Way Home

Rob and Tom are walking home from the spring dance meeting.

"That's too bad about Jessica," says Tom.

"Yeah, it really is," Rob says. "She's such a good kid. It's so tough dealing with all that stuff at home and trying to keep it together yourself. I don't know about you—I thought being 13 was bad, but 14's worse! Most of the time I don't know which end's up. I'd really be going nuts if I had to put up with what she's going through, too."

"Your parents have been divorced for three years?" Tom asks.

"Yes," says Rob. "It seems longer than that. I can hardly remember what it was like when they were married."

"Did you ever think about them getting back together?" Tom asks.

"I did at first," Rob answers. "But Dad moved away even before the divorce was final, so it seemed like a far-fetched idea. I kept wishing for it, though. I remember thinking I'd do anything if we could go back to the way things used to be. I realize now, things don't work like that. You just have to take things the way they are and get on with it. You know, the truth is, things weren't all that great between them for a while before the breakup."

"When did you stop wishing they'd get back together?" Tom asks.

"When Joyce and I got the letter from Dad saying he was getting married, and he enclosed the picture of him and his girlfriend. That was pretty final for me."

"Maybe that's why I don't feel like it's really finished with Mom and Dad," says Tom. "The divorce was final only two months ago, and it still doesn't seem real to me. Maybe it's stupid, but I find myself thinking about them getting back together. Neither of them is dating anyone. That's something I really don't want to think about. How did you feel when you got that letter from your dad?"

"I was really angry," says Rob. "I called him up and told him he'd danced off leaving us behind with the mess while he was just having a great time starting a new life and all. It also upset me to think of him having children with her, replacing Joyce and me. I think what really bothered me, too, was that it made me have to think about Dad sexually. Now, all that seems so long ago. They're really happy together, and Joyce and I have a great time when we visit them. As babies go, Malcolm's the best. I feel like a legend in my own time, the way he follows me around like a puppy."

"Listening to you," Tom says, "makes me think maybe things are going to be OK. I guess I just have to give myself time to get used to it. Well, here's home. I've just made it in time for dinner. There's one other thing I'd like to talk to you about. My father left, just like yours did, and I'm having a real problem with it."

"Sure," Rob says. "Give me a call later tonight. But, you know, the best person to talk to is Darren. He really helped me when I was having such a hard time with it. I'd better get going or *I'll* be late for dinner. Talk to you later."

"Yeah, OK," Tom says. "Thanks, you've helped a lot."

Questions

- Do you fantasize about your parents' getting back together?
- Is it realistic to expect them to?
- Do you think about things you could do to get them together?
- Are they realistic?
- Do you want them back together to make things the way they used to be?
- Describe your home life during the period just before your parents decided to get a divorce.
- Were your parents openly affectionate and considerate with each other?
- Do thoughts of your parents' getting back together get in the way of your accepting the situation as it is and making the best of it?

Someone to Talk To

"Darren! The phone's for you. Don't take too long. I'm expecting a call."

Darren takes the phone, smirking at his sister. "When isn't she expecting a call," he thinks to himself.

"Hello."

"Hello, Darren. This is Tom. Hold on a minute, my ear's recovering. What a voice!"

"Hi, Tom," Darren says. "Yeah, I know. She was bad enough *before* she made the cheerleading squad. Now, we're thinking of getting a lifetime supply of earplugs, or a muzzle. So, what's up?"

"I don't want to bother you. Actually, I really don't know how to start this... I guess I'll just spit it out. Anyway, this is it. I was talking to Rob today about the problems I'm having dealing with my parents' divorce," Tom manages to get out, "and he said I should talk to you. He said you'd helped him a lot."

"I don't know about that, but I guess I was the first in our group to go through a divorce, so, if time counts, I'm it," Darren replies. "Hey, and don't worry about bothering me. Remember, I've been through all this. I know how it feels."

"Thanks, that makes me feel a lot better. Ever since this whole thing started, I can't think about anything else. I feel like I ought to be able to handle it by myself, but I'm going to go nuts if I don't talk about it. That's why it felt so good to talk to Rob. The thing that's really bothering me is how much I miss Dad. I'm having a lot of trouble with that. It's not like he was always around before. But I knew I could count on him when I needed him. Now, I never know where he is. I think I've only talked to him twice since this whole thing started."

"I know how you feel," says Darren. "I was only 9 when Mom and Dad broke up. Dad and I had been real close. We did everything together. That was the hardest thing for me about the divorce. What made it worse was his girlfriend. That's why the whole thing happened in the first place. She was really threatened by Christy and me. I was pulled between needing Dad a lot and being angry at him for doing this to us. It hurt a lot that he chose her over us, me. It was bad."

"I didn't know about all that. It must have been awful. At least I don't have to deal with that yet," Tom replies.

"I won't take you through the early stuff," Darren says. "It was a mess. But there are some things I learned that might make it easier for you. I don't know your situation, but first of all, the best thing you can do for yourself is face the fact of your parents' divorce. I know that's not easy. It took me a long time, but once I stopped struggling and feeling bad and realized this was it, everything got easier. Next, talk to your dad and tell him how you feel, that you need to see him more, talk to him more, whatever, and see if you can work something out together. And, then—this is the hardest part—you just have to wait, let things play out, and give yourself time to get used to the whole thing."

"Darren," Tom says, "what you say makes a lot of sense. What's really clear to me is that I've got to stop just wandering around feeling sorry for myself. You've helped me see I'm not the first person to go through this and that everyone seems to deal with the same kind of stuff. You've given me some good ideas of things I can do. It's up to me. That makes me feel a lot better. Thanks!"

"Hey, great! I'm glad," says Darren. "By now I should be an old hand at this. I'd better get off this phone before we get another earful from Christy. Call me any time you need to talk or whatever."

"Thanks. See you tomorrow."

"Yeah, bye."

Questions

- Do your parents have joint custody of you? That means you spend equal time with both parents.
- If not, which parent do you live with?
- Does your other parent live nearby?

- Do you see and talk with that parent as much as you'd like?
- If not, is there a way to increase your visits by phone or in person?
- When one of your parents moved out of your home, how did you feel?
- Do you have trouble dealing with one of your parents' being away? Or have you come to terms with it?
- Describe your feelings.
- Is there someone you talk to about your feelings?
- Knowing nothing is perfect, what things do you do to help you accept what has happened in your family and make the best of it?

Talking Shop

Rob and Melissa are walking to class.

"Meliss," says Rob, "that's great that you're having the post-dance party."

"At first, I was a little nervous," says Melissa. "I can't believe it's this weekend, but with everybody helping, I should be all right."

"Your mom and stepdad agreed?" asks Rob.

"Oh, yeah. In fact, Bob was more for it than Mom," Melissa answers. "He'd always rather we have things at our house. He's the nicest guy. You know, everything has worked out so well for both my Mom and Dad. It's made it a lot easier for Betsy and me. I just feel so sorry for Jessica."

"Oh," Rob says, "Jessica told me this morning that it looks like her parents have finally decided to get a divorce. I guess that's what that last scene was about."

"Oh, I'm sorry they didn't work it out," says Melissa. "But it's probably better this way, after all they've been through. At least she'll have a lot of us to talk to."

"Yeah, I guess each of us has a story one way or the other," Robert says, laughing.

"Did you ever talk to Tom about his dad?" Melissa asks. "He's having a lot of trouble with that."

"Yes, both Darren and I did," Rob answers. "He said it really helped."

"You know," Melissa says, "everyone seems to have something that's the hardest for them. The worst for me was when Mom started seeing Bob. We'd been just the three of us—Mom, Betsy, and me—for so long. At first, I was really jealous of him taking Mom's time, and I wasn't ready to deal with two older brothers. I liked being the oldest."

"I know," said Rob. "I was just starting to date, and all of a sudden I'm watching my Mom getting all dressed up and going out. It felt strange. It makes you have to look at your parents differently."

"Well," Melissa says, "I was a real brat at first. Part of it was not having Mom all to myself, and part was that I didn't want someone taking Dad's place. It was hard not to like Bob, though. He was so nice and so good-looking. After a while, I could see that it was great for Mom to have someone and that she didn't have to do it all herself. She was a lot happier, too. Dad's around when he can be, and we visit him a lot. So, it's all worked out. To tell you the truth, it's nice having two older stepbrothers and not having Mom watch us like a hawk the way she did before she got married."

"I know what you mean," Rob says. "It takes some getting used to. It's been good for me since my mother got married. She doesn't have to depend on me as much, so I have more time to go out and do things that I want to do. Oh, I almost forgot. We've got a lot of decorations left from last year's party.

Let me know when you want them, and a bunch of us will bring them over and help you put them up."

"Great!" says Melissa. "I was wondering about decorations. How about Friday afternoon after school?"

"That's fine. We'll be there," Rob answers.

"I've got to stop by the office," says Melissa. "See you in class."

"OK," Rob says, "see you later."

Questions

- Are your parents dating new people?
- How does it make you feel?
- Do you feel left out? jealous? other feelings?
- How does the new person treat you?
- Do you feel pulled between liking the new person and still loving your other parent?
- Does the new person in your parent's life have children?
- How do you feel about them?
- Do you do things together as a group?
- Does having the new person in your parent's life take some of the responsibility off you?

Tomorrow "Will Soon Be Here, Better than Today"

The stories you just read are about the issues that young people your age usually have the most trouble with when their parents are getting a divorce:

- Parents battling with each other
- Feelings of loyalty for both parents, or siding with one parent or the other

- The loss of the noncustodial parent
- The parents' new relationships, particularly the custodial parent

Your answers to the questions at the end of each story helped you see how you are dealing with these issues and which ones are the hardest for you.

These issues often cause the feelings listed below. Read through them and notice which ones you feel.

- Fear about what to expect, what is happening, what is going to happen
- Feeling that the changes in the family will disrupt your life: wondering whom you will live with, wondering about having to move, change schools, help more at home, wondering if you will be tied closer to home just when you feel closer ties to your friends and things outside the home
- Fear of what your friends will think, say
- Feeling alone
- Feeling stunned that this could happen
- Feeling relieved that this happened
- Feeling guilty that somehow it's your fault
- Feeling angry at one or both parents
- Feeling pulled between your two parents
- Feeling that one or both parents depend on you too much
- Feeling upset that your parents are dating or getting married again: how it will affect you, whether it's OK to like the new person, whether liking the new person makes you disloyal to your other parent

List other feelings you are having.

A New Perspective

Many teenagers you know, and many more you don't, are going through what you are. Their feelings are the same as yours: fear, anger, sadness, uncertainty.

The young people in the stories are examples of someone like you handling the same things you are. Each person expressed what issue was on his or her mind and how it made him or her feel. Then, either with the help of a friend or on their own, they each were able to understand the problem and work out a way to come to terms with it.

Often, part of the solution is realizing that you need to give yourself time to get used to the changes. No one can do that for you except yourself, and you can't do it for anyone else, whether it's your mother, father, sister, brother, or friend.

You can punish yourself and others with your anger, sadness, or fear, or your feelings of guilt—or you can follow the example of the people in the stories. You can talk your situation over with your friends, think it out on your own, look at your life as it is now—with all its goods and bads—and come to terms with it. As you decide to make the best of it, you will find that you are feeling better about the situation and yourself.

Summary

The uncertainty that comes with your parents' divorce can damage your self-confidence if you let it. Any normal 13- or 14-year-old is already asking: "Who am I, and what am I?" Now the uncertainty and changes are happening on the outside as well. Use the following exercises, and make up some of your own, to help build confidence in yourself. The key is thinking and doing things that make you feel good about who you are and what you are doing.

Self-Esteem Exercises

- Make a list of what you're afraid of, and then make a list of how you can resolve some of these fears.
- Make a list of whom you can talk to about the things you're afraid of that you can't solve on your own.
- If possible, talk to your father about the divorce and ask him what changes he expects to happen.
- If possible, have the same conversation with your mother.
- Talk to a friend whose parents are divorced.
- Make a list of what you're proud of and what you do well. Everything counts—little things as well as big things.
- Spend time with your best friends.
- Make sure to spend time with people you respect and who make you feel good about yourself.
- Make time each day to do something you enjoy that you do well.
- Find a healthy way to let off steam.

Chapter 5
Middle Adolescence
(AGES 15–17)

"I've Got a Real Bad Case of Restless"
—FROM "NEW BLOOD," BY ROBERT CRAY, BRUCE BROMBERG, RICHARD COUSINS, AND PETER BOC

Instructions

Most young people are naturally restless during their teenage years, because their hormonal energy is at an all-time high. When a divorce occurs, the normal energy level spikes even higher, as just about everything in their life turns upside down and becomes uncertain.

This chapter is written just for you and people your age to help you deal with your parents' divorce. By putting names to the feelings you're struggling with and pinpointing the issues that you're troubled by, you will be able to cope more effectively with this experience without long-term effects.

The stories at the beginning of the chapter are about young people like you whose parents are getting a divorce. The stories highlight the feelings and issues you may be confronted with. At the end of each story and throughout the chapter there are questions for you to answer to help you apply the material to your own situation. As you continue through the chapter, there is additional information to help you handle your parents' divorce successfully. Use a separate sheet of paper for your answers.

You may want to share this chapter with your parents or with someone else whose advice you trust. You may want to read and work on it by yourself. You choose what works best for you.

A Sign on the School Bulletin Board

SUPPORT GROUP

- Who? Young people between the ages of 15 and 17 whose parents are going through a divorce.
- What? An open discussion of common experiences and concerns with your peers.
- Where? Room 205.
- When? Every Wednesday afternoon from 4 to 6 P.M.

The First Meeting: Getting Started

Twelve young people are sitting in a circle. Some are talking among themselves, others are looking around waiting for something to happen, all are exhibiting varying degrees of nervousness.

"Hey, whose idea was this, anyway?" asks Jack.

Ron and Claire start to speak at once.

"Go ahead," says Ron.

"OK," says Claire. "Ron and I were talking the other day about our parents' divorces and what we were dealing with. The more we talked, the more we realized we were having many of the same experiences, and talking about them really helped us both. So, we thought, why not see if others would like to get together and do the same thing on a regular basis? It was Ron's idea to put the note on the bulletin board just to see if anyone else was interested. That way, no one would feel put on the spot by being asked directly, and we wouldn't feel weird just walking up to someone and sticking our nose in their business. So, here we are."

"We don't have any organized plan," Ron continues. "Our idea was just to see if anyone turned up and then decide, as a group, how we wanted it to work."

The students spend the next hour putting together a plan for the group. A list is drawn up of discussion topics. Each week a topic will be on the table. Everyone will take turns talking about his or her experience with the topic and then will either make suggestions about how he or she dealt with the issue or ask for suggestions from the group.

"Ron and Claire, this is a great idea," says Greg. "I never would have talked about my parents' divorce and the problems I'm having with it, otherwise. I never realized so many of us are going through the same stuff."

"Yeah," Stacey agrees. "I pretty much felt I had to keep it to myself, like it was embarrassing or something. I like the idea of picking the topic ahead. Then we have a week to think about it."

"I like that idea, too," says Nick. "But what if something happens during the week that's really urgent for one of us? How about at the beginning of each meeting we check to see if anyone has something that needs talking about, give them a chance to discuss it, and then go on to the topic we've chosen?"

Everyone nods, agreeing that that's a good idea.

Then Sharon says, "One thing worries me. Some of us are more comfortable talking than others. Part of what's so good about this idea is that we're all together having the chance to get stuff off our chests. It would be too bad if the ones who are more comfortable talking end up doing all the talking and the others are left out."

"That's a good point," Jack agrees. "I guess we'll just have to notice for ourselves if we're rambling on or if we're not taking an active part. Another thought I had was to include kids whose parents' divorce is already final. They might still be having trouble with the same things we are, or maybe they will have figured out a way to work them out."

"Yeah, that's a great idea," Claire says. "Why don't we put up another notice? Anybody want to do it?"

"Sure, I will," Jack answers. "I'll do it tomorrow."

"Any other ideas or suggestions?" Greg asks. "I don't want to miss anything, but I've got to get going. I promised Mom I'd pick up Patricia, and I'm already late."

"I just want to thank Claire and Ron for coming up with this idea," Sharon says. "I never would have thought of it."

"It helps just to get together like this and see how we're dealing with the same things," adds someone else.

"Guess that's it, then."

"See you around."

Questions

- Is there someone you talk to about the things you're dealing with concerning your parents' divorce?
- Does it help to talk about these things?
- Is it hard for you to discuss them with someone?
- Do you have friends whose parents have gotten a divorce or are getting one?
- Do you find you're dealing with the same things?
- Have your friends given you some ideas of how to handle the things that are bothering you?
- Have you given them some suggestions to help them?

- Do you think it would help you to have a group like the one in the story?
- If you haven't talked about the issues that are bothering you, do you think it would be helpful to you if you did?

The Second Meeting: Getting into It

It's the following Wednesday and the topic is "The Most Difficult Thing for You to Deal with About the Divorce." To make sure everyone has a chance to talk, each person has taken a number as they come into the room. Sharon has drawn #1 and begins to speak.

"First, is there anything urgent anyone wants to bring up?" she asks.

"Yeah," says Nick, "does anybody have any idea what Mr. Hirano was talking about in geometry today?"

After a few chuckles, everyone settles down.

"Well, if there isn't any other urgent issue, I guess I'll get started. I had trouble picking just one thing that bothers me. I finally decided they all kind of fall into a broad category. I'm really having trouble with what I thought my family was, what I wanted it to be, and what it is. Does that make any sense?"

"Yeah, I know what you mean," says Ron. "It's like this kind of thing happens to somebody else, but I never thought it would happen to me."

"That's sort of what I mean, but not quite," Sharon says. "In my mind, I have this picture of how a family is supposed to be. It's not like our family was perfect before or anything like that—we had our problems; who doesn't?—but we were a family. It was there and always would be for me to fall back on, count on. Now it feels like it's all over the place. It's not like the picture at all."

"I think I know what you mean," says Stacey. "To me, it's like there are two pictures. When I think about who I am, there's the one I'm supposed to be and the one I am. Some parts of the pictures are the same, some aren't, and it seems to be constantly changing. Same with my family: There was the picture family and the real family. My real family maybe wasn't exactly like the picture family before, but now it isn't like it at all."

"Yeah," Sharon nods. "And there's more to it than that, for me. It's something about the difference between the person I was five years ago and the person I'm becoming now, the family as it was before the divorce, and the family it's turning into. I feel completely confused all the time between the real and the ideal and the way everything keeps changing."

"I feel the same way," Greg says, "if I understand what you're saying. What's hard for me about what's happening is that everything's changing all at once. I'm having to adjust to all the changes I feel in myself, which is confusing enough. Now I'm in the middle of a family that's all mixed up, too. I don't know what my family is anymore, and I sure don't know where it's going. My real family, whatever that is, isn't a thing like any picture family—and where do I fit in, in all of this?"

"You know," Jack begins, "at first, nothing anyone was saying made any sense to me. Then I realized you were describing just what I've been feeling but hadn't been able to put into words. I've just been feeling so confused and mixed up since this whole divorce thing got started. I couldn't put my finger on what was causing it. Talking like this has really helped me understand what's been going on with me."

Several others nod, as Sharon says, "Hey, I just realized what time it is. It's almost six already. I feel bad about taking up the whole time."

"You didn't. Everyone had a chance to talk," says Nick. "It worked out perfectly. We took your problem and said how it applied to ourselves. Each of us had our own angle on it. It seemed to me everyone was getting something out of the discussion and adding something to it."

"I guess," Claire continues, "dealing with the divorce is just going to continue to be confusing until we get used to how our families sort things out. After listening to all of us talk, it helps me to know it's not just me, that there's nothing wrong with me."

"Yeah," Nick says, "nothing wrong that isn't wrong with every other teenager just trying to grow up in this crazy world."

"Now that Nick's given us all his seal of approval, I guess we'll survive after all," Stacey says with a laugh. Everyone joins in and heads for the door.

Questions

- Has the divorce made you feel "confused and mixed up" like the young people in the story?
- What do you think caused these feelings for you?
- Do you have trouble with the difference between the picture you have in your mind of how a family ought to be and how your family is?
- Do you have difficulty figuring out where you fit?
- What is the hardest thing for you to deal with about the divorce?
- Do you talk to someone about the things that bother you?

The Third Meeting: Rick's Turn

Another week has gone by and Rick begins the session by saying, "I think Claire suggested today's topic, 'Wishing Our Parents Would Get Back Together.' I hadn't thought about that until she brought it up. Now I realize it's been in the back of my mind, too. I've always liked to think of my family being together doing things, like Christmas, going on trips, things like that."

"Yeah, I feel the same way," says Stacey, "but it's more than that for me. All of us here are 15, 16, or 17. I don't know about you, but I'm having enough trouble working on my own stuff. Now I have all this to deal with, too. I wish they'd just figure out how to get along with each other so we could all be back together again."

"I guess part of me would like to see my parents back together, too," says Michael. "In some ways, it sure would be easier on me, but I remember what it was like before, when they were together. Sometimes it was really bad."

"Maybe I was too wrapped up in my own stuff," says Jack. "But I didn't notice any problems between Mom and Dad. They just announced one day they were getting divorced. Fine, I guess that's their decision, but now we have to live with it. I feel completely out of it, out of control, everything."

"Jack," says Sharon, "you may feel like you're out of control, but you seem to be handling this better than a lot of us."

"Thanks, Sharon. I guess one thing that helps me a lot is sports. Sometimes I don't know what I would do without them. I can really work off steam and, even better, I know that it's up to me how far I want to go and how well I want to do."

"I know what you mean," Claire says. "I always feel better after I've worked out. I brought up the topic of parents' getting back together because it was something that's been on my mind a lot. I thought if they did, it would make things right again. Listening to everyone's feelings has made me think about it differently. They really didn't get along at all the last few years. And if I'm really being honest, it was awfully hard on me and Blair. I hated all their arguing and fighting and just the cold feeling that was always there. I think of what I want to do with my life, and I realize I would hate to live for the rest of it stuck with someone who wants entirely different things than I do and who I can't get along with even for a few minutes. The only thing my parents seem to have in common is we children, and most of the time they can't seem to agree about that. I guess I'll be all right, once I get used to the way things are now."

"Claire," Ron says, "you sound so sad. I guess we all do, to some degree. You and I have talked a lot about this. What helps me is to think that my parents sure weren't a very good example of what I would want a relationship to be. The more I was around them when it was bad, the more cynical I was about what to expect. What I'd really like to see is this whole divorce thing over with, the two of them with people they can be happy with, so I can get back to worrying about something simple—like what I want to be when I grow up!"

"Ron, I hadn't thought of it quite like that," says Claire. "That helps a lot."

"Yeah, me too," Nick says. "I was feeling the same as Claire, but I was afraid to admit it."

"I can't believe it," Rick says. "Time's up already. These meetings sure go fast. Usually I can't sit still for more than fifteen minutes max before I start fidgeting. I was nervous at first about being here. Now I really look forward to the next time." The others nod, agreeing, and the meeting breaks up.

Questions

- What was your parents' behavior like toward each other before the divorce?
- How do they treat each other now?
- Do you think about them getting back together?
- What are the reasons you'd like them to get back together?
- What do think are the chances of that happening?

- Were they an example for you of a good relationship before the divorce?
- What are the qualities you'd like to have in your own relationships?

The Fourth Meeting: The Missing Parent

It's the following Wednesday, and the discussion begins with Greg saying, "I don't know about everyone else, but I've really had trouble with Dad's moving out. Mom and Dad spent a lot of time talking and explaining to Lauren, Todd, and me, but nothing much was happening. Then one day I came home from school and Dad was gone. That's when the divorce got real for me. It was like there was a big hole where he used to be."

"Yeah," joins in Nick, "once I got used to the idea of a divorce and stopped wondering what people were going to think, it really sank in that Dad wasn't going to be around like he used to be. It bothered me a lot. I called him up and we talked a long time about it. Actually, as it turns out, we probably spend more time doing things together now than we used to."

"You're lucky," Stacey says. "My Dad has moved away. It's like he's just evaporated. Mom talks to us about it, trying to help us feel better, but it's going to take me a while to get used to it—if I ever do. It makes this whole thing even harder. I can't help but think somehow it's my fault or there's something wrong with me and he doesn't want us, me, anymore."

"You know, Stacey," says Michael, "I think we all feel the same as you do, some of us more than others. Karen, my sister, really helped me with that. She said Dad's probably kept away from us because seeing us and talking to us reminds him of what he's lost and he isn't big enough to deal with that yet, if he ever will be. She also reminded me the trouble was and is between Mom and Dad. We didn't make this happen, even though we sure have to deal with the results."

"That's probably true," agrees Claire. "But can't they see that their not having anything to do with us makes the loss real? We're missing and hurting just like they are. I wish I were still angry at Dad like I was when he first left. That made it a whole lot easier. Now I just miss him."

"At first," Sharon says, "I was going through the same thing. I finally called Dad and told him pretty much what you just said, Claire. And I also told him it was stupid for all of us to be trying to deal with the missing and hurting alone when we could talk about it together and help each other. Then Dad said the best thing. He said I'd helped him already by getting him to see that we were still a family. We were his children and he was our Dad, whether we lived under the same roof or not. After that, I haven't felt so empty."

"I wish I felt more empty," Rick says. "Since Dad left, it's like Mom expects me to take care of all the things Dad used to do. I know she also leans a lot on Cammie, emotionally. It's a good thing it's Cammie. I don't have much patience with that. Sometimes I wish I could just walk away and not have to deal with all this. But then after I've had a good case of feeling sorry for myself, it's like I get a second wind and I realize we all have to stick together and pitch in to help each other. Being here with all of you has really helped me keep it together. Everyone is talking about the same things I'm thinking about, and I can say how I feel without feeling funny about it. Best of all, being here, doing this, really helps me let off steam."

"That sure sums it up for me," says Jack. "Speaking of new chores, Mom's working late, so I've got to pick up stuff for dinner. Any suggestions?" And another session is over.

Questions

- How soon did one of your parents move out of the house?
- Did your parents discuss it with you first?

- How did you feel when it happened?
- How do you feel about it now?
- Do you see or talk to the parent who left as much as you'd like?
- Do you feel the divorce was somehow your fault?
- Do you feel you've had to fill the void for the parent who left? In what ways?
- Have you been able to talk over your feelings with the parent who left? with the parent you live with?
- Who are your role models?
- How do you let off steam?

The Fifth Meeting: Jack Brings Up Something Urgent

It's a week later and, as everyone is finding a seat, Jack asks, "Would anybody mind if I go first? Something happened this week that I really need to talk about."

Everyone shakes their head, "No," so Jack continues.

"Mom has started dating, and it looks pretty serious. She and Dad are legally separated and don't seem to have a problem with it, but I feel uncomfortable. Who is this guy, anyway?"

"I know the feeling," Michael says. "I guess my parents have been separated longer than yours. Mom's been dating for a while. In fact, so has Dad. In the beginning, I felt sort of protective about her, now that I'm the 'man' of the house. I almost felt like I should wait up for her, like I was the parent, a chaperone or something. Then it changed, and I wasn't keeping track of several of them, till it got to be that she was only seeing Jeff. They're seeing each other really a lot, spending weekends together—everything. My sister and I have talked a lot about it. It's like the roles are reversed. I'm not sure I'm comfortable thinking about my mother like that."

"The whole reason my parents broke up to begin with," Claire says, "is because of a man Mom works with. It was awful when Dad found out. We've been dealing with that, on top of everything else. At least your parents didn't do that. I realize now that if things had been good between Mom and Dad, another person couldn't have gotten between them. It's taken me a long time to realize that, though. At first, I was so angry at Mom that I refused to talk to her and wanted to live with Dad."

"I had just the opposite situation," Greg says. "Dad left Mom for a woman who didn't want anything to do with us. Dad has had to choose between his children and her, and he's being really unfair to Mom about money. I don't know how everything's going to end up, but it's a good thing Dad has moved pretty far away; otherwise, we'd all be in the middle of World War III all the time. As it is, long distance keeps the volume down."

Ron says, "Mom and Dad haven't started dating yet, as far as I know. What a bitch. Everything is turned upside down. Just when you think you've got one thing sorted out, something else comes up. I hadn't really thought about the 'Dating Stage.' I guess I'm glad you brought this up, Jack. As they say, forewarned is forearmed."

"Life used to be so simple," Sharon says. "I used to worry about good grades, whether I had plans for Saturday night, and what I wanted to do after high school. Now I'm wondering if we're going to have to move, who Dad is going to go out with, and whether there'll be enough money for me to go to college."

"I guess it just shows what you can deal with when you have to," says Stacey. "I sure am glad I have you to talk to. Hey, Jack, if you have any more bombshells, could you keep them to yourself?...Just kidding."

Everyone laughs and the meeting begins to break up.

Questions

- Are your parents dating?
- Was there another person who triggered your parents' divorce?
- How do you feel about your parents' dating?
- Has another person in your parent's life come between you and your parent?
- Do you feel jealous, protective, or happy about someone new in your parent's life?
- How does the other parent talk or behave about the parent who is dating?
- How does one parent behave and talk about the new person in the other parent's life?
- Are you picking up your behavior from theirs?
- Is your parent's new relationship a better example of what a good relationship can be: supportive, affectionate, happy, fun?
- Thinking back over the stories you just read, answer the following questions.
  - — What situations discussed in the stories apply to you?
  - — What other issues upset you?
  - — Describe how each of the situations you're dealing with makes you feel.
  - — What have you done about them so far?
  - — Whom can you talk to about these things?
  - — Whom do you feel closest to in your family?

Going a Step Further

The feelings and issues the young people discussed in the stories you've just read are a good beginning for looking at your own. Now you need to go a step further. The combination of your own growing-up issues and the changes caused by your parents' divorce can be emotionally very intense and very uncomfortable for you. Your feelings are your own—neither bad nor good—but no one likes to feel out of control. Recognizing your feelings and understanding what causes them can help you bring them under control and help you feel better about yourself.

Let's look at the feelings young people your age usually deal with during their parents' divorce. Fear is a very common feeling at such times. Feelings of uncertainty and insecurity can cause tremendous anxiety for young people, as they wonder what's going to happen to them and where they fit in. Feeling that it's up to them to make things right can add to the burden.

Feeling helpless to do anything about the divorce can make young people feel depressed and out of control.

They may feel a great deal of anger—anger at the divorce for "ruining everything" as well as anger at their parents for causing the divorce to happen, for messing up their life, and for not being and behaving the way they think parents should.

Young people may feel the divorce is their fault and may feel guilty about their feelings toward one or both of their parents.

All of these feelings undermine self-esteem. A young person might think, "I feel useless, helpless, and out of control. I am unlovable. I'm not OK. It doesn't matter what I do or don't do. It won't make any difference. I'm tired of it all. I don't feel like doing anything. Everyone's better than I am."

Now, let's look at the issues that divorce and parental behavior may produce. A damaged self-esteem undermines a sense of security and the ability to have easy, healthy relationships. Self-image with friends is low, and relationships with members of the family are strained.

With the family breaking up, it's difficult for the young person to know what's going to happen and what's expected of him or her.

Instead of using the home as a solid base and moving out and expanding beyond the family, the young person may either stay at home more than usual, feeling safer there, or rush away from the confusion at home to seek a haven elsewhere.

Friends—an important source of involvement and support—may be avoided because of embarrassment about what's going on at home.

It is normal for you to feel a growing sense of responsibility for yourself and the world around you. The divorce may cause you either to take on more responsibility than is appropriate, both at home and outside, or to withdraw and not carry out minimal responsibilities.

Most young people have little or no patience for conflict outside themselves as they try to cope with their own internal confusion growing up. Witnessing parental warfare and, even worse, being pulled into the middle of the conflict is particularly disturbing.

A parent's new romantic interest is awkward for a young person who is grappling with his or her own sexuality.

Parental authority under ordinary conditions is questioned. Because of the divorce, the young person is even more resistant to it. Any such interference by a new person in the parent's life is impossible to accept.

Society's rules and institutions, normally tested by young people, are further undermined in their eyes by the divorce. Their faith is shaken in adults in general, in parents in particular, and in other things like "home," "marriage," and so on.

Questions

- Which feelings have you had the most difficulty with?
- Which issues have been hardest for you?
- What are the hardest ones for you to talk about? Whom would you discuss these with?
- What are the best things about being your age? the worst?
- What do you like most about your family? What are the things about your family that make you angry? that you don't like? that embarrass you?
- What are some good things coming out of the divorce?
- Do your parents make you angry? Make a list of how your dad makes you angry. Make a list of how your mom makes you angry.
- Think of three things you like about your mom; about your dad. If you can, try to keep these in mind when you get angry at them.

Putting It All Together

The issues the young people brought up in the stories at the beginning of the chapter are examples of what every person your age is concerned with when a divorce happens. Your family, like theirs, is in chaos just when you most need its security and predictability to help you cope with the normal problems and confusion of growing up.

It's natural to feel anger and sadness and to ask, "Why does this have to happen to me?" You did not cause the divorce, but you are stuck, just the same, with its effects and the changes it causes in your life. You do have the power to decide how you are going to react to the changes caused by the divorce and your parents' behavior. You can decide to let the divorce overwhelm you and use it as a permanent excuse for your shortcomings and failures and blame it for everything that's wrong with your life. Or, you can decide to continue to learn the skills you need to become an independent and responsible person and to develop the confidence in yourself to make the choices that are best for you.

There will be times when you feel discouraged or confused, when you don't like yourself, your parents, or your life very much. These are all normal emotions with or without divorce. You are in good company.

Everyone your age is dealing with the same problems and concerns that come with growing up. Many, just like you, are dealing with their parents' divorce, as well. Some may appear to be handling the stresses and strains of adolescence better than others, but below the surface everyone shares the same confusions, doubts, and fears. If you believe that you have the concern and love of your parents, or, in some cases, one parent, that you can do well in school, that you have friends to share good times with, you will.

Divorce can be an experience you take in your stride. You can use it to learn how to deal with other crises that are bound to come along and move forward, confident in a happy and fulfilling life of which you can be proud.

Summary

List the growing-up issues that are hardest for you. How have they been affected by your parents' divorce? How do they make you feel and act?

Frequent Concerns During Divorce and Afterward

- Parents' battling with each other
- Feeling loyalty divided between parents
- Loss of time with noncustodial parent

- Taking care of parents' emotional burdens
- Parents' new relationships

Self-Esteem Exercises

- Choose a friend you feel close to, and plan something to do together.
- Think of something you do well, and remember to make time for it when you're feeling upset.
- Allow yourself to take pride in and spend time on things that you do well and that make you feel good about yourself. Allow yourself to stop outside activities that add to your stress and make it hard for you to take care of yourself.
- What do you like most about yourself?
- What word would your friends use to describe you? What word would your parents use? your teachers use? you yourself use?
- What are your favorite things to do by yourself? when you're with friends?
- What's your favorite time of day, and why? day of the week, and why?
- Imagine your ideal life, and describe your family and yourself; where you'd live, what things you'd be doing, and whom you'd do them with. Include people, things, and activities you like that are already in your life. Think of ways to bring some more of your "ideal" life into your "real" life.
- Give yourself credit for doing the best you can do in this situation, leaving the responsibility of the divorce to your parents.

Chapter 6
Late Adolescence
(AGES 18–19)

"Many Rivers to Cross
but I Can't Seem to Find My Way Over"
—Jimmy Cliff

Instructions

At 18 and 19, young people are making real strides emotionally and physically to separate from their family. When divorce occurs, the family separates within itself, taking away the solid base from which the young person is preparing to launch.

This chapter is written just for you to help you recognize and work through the very special issues that divorce causes for young people your age. It will put names to the feelings you are wrestling with and pinpoint the concerns you are or will be dealing with, so that you can move smoothly through this period of your life with no lasting ill effects.

The stories in the chapter are composites about young people confronting the same feelings and issues with their parents' divorce that you are. At the end of each story and throughout the chapter are questions for you to answer that will make the material more meaningful for you in your situation. Use a separate sheet for your answers. As you continue through the chapter, additional information is given to help you successfully handle the divorce at this stage of your life.

You may want to share this chapter with someone, or you may want to read and work on it by yourself. You choose what works best for you.

Many Rivers to Cross

The town career center is holding its Spring Career Fair. Young people are milling around, learning about job opportunities and careers.

"Jan," says Dana, "I didn't know you were in town."

"Oh, hi, Dana," Jan says. "It's college spring break and I've got to find a job for this summer, so here I am. Hey, look—there are Kate, Clarke, and Ben."

"Yeah, I was just talking to Liz and Neil. They're here, too," Dana says. "It's like a reunion!"

"Are you looking for a job, too?" Jan asks. "I thought you were all set to get your degree in computer programming."

"Well," Dana answers, "I was—I mean, I am. I guess you didn't hear that my parents got a divorce. Since Dad's remarried, he's really involved with his new family. Our money situation was never great, but now it's awful. So I've got to get a job to support my night school."

"Hey, I'm sorry," says Jan. "That's got to make it hard. How can you be so calm about it? I'd be real mad."

"Actually, it's better now that they're divorced than before, when they were married and fighting all the time. Also, I always had a job of one kind or another during high school, so it's really nothing new. The difference is, this way, I can take credit for giving myself this education. I don't have to worry whether there's going to be money for it. It's up to me, and that really makes me feel good."

"Hi, Dana. Hi, Jan," Jamie breaks in. "I just overheard what you were saying, Dana. I'm kind of in the same boat. My parents have just started going through a divorce. I don't know if I'm coming or going, but I do know one thing: I'm getting a job this summer to get me out of that house. It's awful. In fact, I was just talking to Ben and we're thinking of getting an apartment together. If you hear of anyone else who's looking for a place, let me know. The more ways we split it up, the better."

"Jamie," Dana says, "I'm sorry to hear that. I remember how hard it was on me when my parents were going through all that. Why am I saying, 'my parents'? We were *all* going through all that."

"Wait a minute, Jamie," Jan says. "I was just talking to Neil last night, and he was talking about looking for a place for the summer. Actually, probably for longer than that. He says he's not going back to college in the fall. Why don't you give him a call?"

"Thanks, I'll do that. Isn't it great seeing everybody? We've all scattered, over the last year or so. Why don't we get everyone together and catch up? I'd offer my house, but no telling what'll be going on there."

"I know Mom and Dad would love to see everyone again," Jan says. "How about my house?"

"That's terrific," Dana says. "I'll help you telephone everybody."

"I'll ask Neil when I talk to him about the apartment," says Jamie. "See you later."

"Yeah, OK."

"Bye."

Questions

- How do you feel about your parents' getting a divorce?
- What is the situation like at home?
- Are you living at home?

- Are you in college, full-time or part-time? in night school?
- How is the divorce affecting your current living status? your plans for school?
- How do you think it will affect them?
- Did you have jobs during high school?
- Do you have a job now?
- How do you think the divorce will affect your job or your need to get a job?
- Does the divorce make you feel you need to be more independent in terms of where you live? in terms of making money? in terms of how you deal with other areas of your life?

A River to Cross

"Hi, Neil. This is Jamie."

"Hi, Jamie," Neil answers. "Didn't I see you at the career center today?"

"Yeah," Jamie laughs. "Me and about a thousand other people, give or take a few. Seems like I ran into just about everyone I know. As a matter of fact, Dana, Jan, and I thought it would be a great idea to get all of us together like old times and catch up with what everybody's doing. Jan says we can have it at her house. What do you think?"

"I don't know," says Neil. "I think I have a crack at filling in for one of the waiters down at Joe's. If I get the chance, I have to do it. I really need the money. I'm moving out of the house as soon as I can find an apartment, and I'll need all the help I can get."

"That's the other reason I called," says Jamie. "I've got to find a place, too. I guess there's no reason to beat around the bush with you. We've known each other forever. My parents are getting a divorce. They dropped the news on us last night. Not like it was a surprise. It's been coming for a long time, but the last six months have been the worst: arguing, fighting, pulling Janet, Whitney, and me into it whenever we were around, even physical stuff. As the other male in the house, I always felt I had to protect Mom. At the same time, I could see what she did that made Dad get mad. I was so upset and mixed up, I thought I was going crazy. Now that it's finally happened, it's a relief. I've really lost respect for both of them. I can't believe my parents are behaving like this. I feel bad about moving out, but I've got to get on with my own life. I've already told Mom I'll come over and help her out when I can, but I can't take living there anymore. It's time anyway. I am 19 years old, after all."

"Jamie, don't feel like you have to explain to me. I'm trying to find a way to cross the same river you are," Neil says. "My parents have been separated since before we finished high school. It just went on and on. Over Christmas, things came to a head and they finally decided to get a divorce. Then they really got into it. Money was the big issue, and my college tuition was right at the top of the list. Who was going to pay for it? It was like they were trading baseball cards—one college tuition for one something else. I felt like I was the thing being traded back and forth. So, I said 'Forget it, I'm out of here. Go play with somebody else's marbles.' Who needs it? I think I've got it worked out. I'll finish this year at school—it's paid for—then find a place of my own, make my own money, get a student loan, and go from there. That's my plan, anyway. We'll see how it goes. But until they start acting like adults, I'm keeping my distance. The hard thing is, I really love them both, but they've got to sort out their own stuff without me. Poor Lindsay is still in there fighting, talking first to one of them and then the other, back and forth. Not me. I've finally gotten over a lot of the anger. Now, I'm just trying to hold on to my love for them, but one more of those scenes and that will be gone, too."

"You have really been through it," Jamie says. "I guess one way or the other, no matter whose family it is or divorce it is, we all end up dealing with pretty much the same things. Looks like we both need a place; so does Ben. I've got a couple of listings. You want to go check them out tonight? I've got to say, it's a relief to think about my own stuff for a change, instead of what does my family stand for and when are my parents going to grow up."

"Yeah," Neil chuckles. "I know what you mean and I'm glad we can still laugh. I've got some leads, too. See if you can get hold of Ben and we can take a look at them together, tonight, after work."

"Sounds good to me," Jamie says. "Actually, I'm looking forward to being out on my own. It'll be a lot of fun, especially with you and Ben. See you tonight."

Questions

- How long were your parents separated before they began divorce proceedings?
- How did they treat each other during that time?
- How are they treating each other during the divorce?
- How does their behavior make you feel?
- Do they put you in the middle?
- Do you feel you have to take sides?
- Do you feel disloyal to one when you are with the other?
- Do they expect you to act as a go-between or a source of information about the other?
- Describe your feelings about your mother and about your father.
- Is there someone you talk to or can talk to about your feelings and what's happening?

One River at a Time

"Ben, it's Liz."

"Hi, Liz," says Ben. "Am I glad you called! I really need to talk. Sometimes this home situation is more than I can take."

"Hey, that's part of what I love about our relationship. We can always talk to each other about what's bothering us. Tell me what happened. You sound really upset," says Liz.

"Well, I just had a big scene with Mom," Ben answers. "It all started when I said I was going with Jamie and Neil to look at some apartments. Oh, did Jan talk to you about Saturday night?"

"Yeah, she did," Liz answers. "I think it sounds like fun. Want to go?"

"Sounds good to me," Ben says. "It'll be great to see everyone. We've all been so spread out since graduation. Anyway, back to Mom. She starts in with, 'This is a perfectly good home. Why do you want to live somewhere else?' Then she goes on about how much she needs me around to help her out with the other kids and other stuff. Like all this is my responsibility."

"Where did that come from? She's known you were planning to move out for months," Liz says.

"I know," says Ben. "I guess it's one thing to talk about it, another to see it really happening. I don't know, really. Part of it is, I think she had a bad time at court today. She and Dad are really fighting this thing out. Well, Mom and I went on for a while, mainly with her going on about how unfair Dad was and how hard everything was on her, that she was a human being, and didn't she have a right to some happiness. That's when I lost it and said, no, she didn't, if it made everybody else unhappy, that she was a mother and it was up to her to make everything right, fix it with Dad, and get us back together as a family. I feel really bad about what I said. I really upset her, I know. She just looked at me for the longest time and then walked out of the room."

"Oh, Ben," Liz sympathizes. "I know you must feel awful, and that's not even what you really think."

"I feel real stupid saying this," Ben says. "But sometimes I feel just like a little kid who wishes this divorce didn't have to happen, that it would all just go away, that Mom could make everything right and put everything back together again. I know that's not how it is, that it's just a fantasy. She has a right to make her life the way she wants it. I just wish it didn't have to be so hard on all of us, and I really wish she didn't depend on me so much. That's why I feel I have to get my own place."

"I don't blame your mom," Liz says. "I count on you, too. You make it so easy."

"Yeah, but with you and me, we both help each other and, anyway, it's a different situation entirely," says Ben. "You know, if I didn't have the experience of our relationship, I'd really wonder if good relationships were possible."

"I know," Liz says. "We've both felt that way. It's strange, but in a funny way I think seeing our parents' relationships fall apart and hearing that our friends are going through the same thing, we won't take relationships for granted. You and I have certainly talked a lot about what a good relationship involves, and maybe that's why. For us, at least, our parents' divorces have taught us what we don't want and have shown us how valuable a good relationship is."

"Hey, that's a new twist—divorce your way to better relationships," Ben says with a laugh. "Just teasing. Maybe I'm not, though. Maybe you've got something there. I guess I'd better go see if I can patch things up with Mom. Now that I've talked it out, I can see I really was pretty infantile. Thanks for listening. I always feel better when we talk and I can get stuff off my chest."

"Hey, it just happened to be your turn this time. It works both ways," Liz says. "Let me know how the apartments look."

"It'll probably be too late tonight when I get back. Want a ride to campus tomorrow? We both have 10 o'clock classes. We can stop for coffee at College Center and talk about them."

"Sounds great," says Liz. "See you then."

Questions

- How has your relationship been with your father during the divorce? with your mother?
- Do you feel either or both of them depend on you too much?
- Do you blame one of them for breaking up the family? If so, which one, and why?
- Do you think about them getting back together?
- Do you think, with a divorce, you can have good relationships with family members? Do you have good relationships with the members of your family?
- Whom are you closest to in your family?
- Whom do you talk to in your family about your feelings? outside of your family?
- Was your parents' relationship an example of the kind of relationship you want?
- Describe the relationship you want to have.

Other Rivers to Cross

"Kate, it's Dana."

"Oh, hi, Dana. I was just thinking about you," Kate says.

"All good things, I hope," Dana laughs. "I picked up a lot of pamphlets at the Spring Career Fair, and I got some extras for you that I thought you'd be interested in."

"Oh, that's great," says Kate. "You really saved my life saying you were going. I was looking forward to it. There hasn't been a lot of time to think about a job at school, and the college career center there is completely worthless. This Career Fair was going to be my big chance to get going on it and then, at the last moment, I couldn't go."

"Hey, Kate, is something the matter?" Dana asks. "You don't sound like yourself."

"Yeah, I'd say something's the matter," Kate says. "It's this whole thing with Mom and Dad. The family's just a mess."

"Want to talk about it?" Dana asks.

"I guess so," Kate answers. "You know, it's funny, even though I've been away at college and you've stayed here and we haven't really seen each other much since high school, I still feel like you're my best friend and the person I feel closest to. Also, you've been through this whole divorce thing, so you understand what I'm dealing with. It's not so embarrassing talking to you about it."

"I was thinking the other day," Dana says, "that my family was probably the first in our group to break up, but, you know, now that I think about the people we were closest to in high school, only Clarke's and Jan's families are still together. So, what's been bothering you? I hate to hear you so down. You're always the one who keeps everyone else up."

"Well, it was bad enough when Mom and Dad couldn't get their act together," says Kate. "Were they just separated or were they getting a divorce? One day it was one way and the next day it was the other. We kids didn't know whether we were packing our bags or hanging our pictures back up. Mom and Dad were clear about one thing, though: If they got a divorce, we'd for sure have to move. So, every time I opened a new tube of toothpaste I wondered if I'd finish it in my old bathroom or throw it away in a new one. Does that sound funny? Plus, I really miss Steve. With him away, I feel responsible for the other kids."

"No, that doesn't sound funny," Dana says. "I felt the same way. Actually, I'm still not sure how long we'll be in this house. We may have to move, too. You get used to not knowing after a while, and you concentrate on things you can do something about."

"It's good to know I'm not so strange after all," Kate says. "Anyway, now everything has picked up on the divorce front because—are you ready for this one?—Mom has fallen in love! Can you believe that? After twenty-four years of marriage, four, count 'em, four children, the oldest of whom is about to graduate from college and get married himself, Mom is like a 15-year-old, all starry-eyed, dancing around. Who's the mother here, and who's the kid? And worse, 'Heartthrob's' son is hitting on *me* and I can't *stand* him! My God, he's only 15. His voice hasn't even changed yet. What a joke! I can't bear any of this. I don't even know if I'll be able to go to Jan's on Saturday. We're supposed to have a two-family get-together so that we can all get to 'know' each other. Dad's having a fit, now that he doesn't have Mom's undivided attention with his backing and forthing about the divorce. It's a nut-house over here. When the phone rings, I don't know which to prepare for: 'Katherine, put your mother on the phone,' or 'Well, hello, Kate. How are you? Your mother and I are going to the movies tonight, and we'd love you and the other children to go with us.' Right!"

Dana, laughing, says, "I'm sorry, Kate. I shouldn't laugh, but you make it sound so funny. Well, you know, younger men are the rage now. You're just a woman of your time and you know you're irresistible."

Now Kate is laughing, too. "How is it that every time I talk to you, somehow I always end up feeling better?" she asks. "And you're right. I guess I am irresistible. Poor kid doesn't have a chance. Actually, once he fills out and stops sounding like a boy soprano, he may not be half bad! Seriously, with things the way they are, I can't count on much here. I really have to get a job lined up for this summer. On the other hand, the way things are going, I could make a fortune babysitting. What am I saying? I knew I was going around the bend. Dana, you've got the right idea about having a real job. It would sure help me feel more on my own and like I have some control over the situation."

"Yeah," says Dana, "it's always made me feel more independent, plus it's something to concentrate on and think about when your family is getting to you. So, what do you want to do about Saturday? I'd hate for you to miss seeing everyone."

"Well, I guess I can't get out of 'The Family Get to Know Each Other' gathering completely," Kate says, "so probably I'll stay through dinner, then go over to Jan's after."

"That's great. I didn't want to miss seeing you," Dana says. "I'll be sure to bring the pamphlets."

"Thanks a lot, Dana, for being such a good friend. See you Saturday," Kate says.

"Sure," Dana says. "You know, you've helped me, telling me about your mother's new relationship. I haven't had to deal with that yet. Guess I'll cross that one when I get to it."

"Hey, anything I can do to help," Kate says. "I should be a pro by then! See you Saturday."

Questions

- Have your school or job plans been affected by your parents' getting a divorce?
- Do you feel you have to take more responsibility in your family or for yourself because of the divorce?
- During the divorce, how has your parents' behavior changed toward you? toward the other children in your family? toward each other? in general?
- How has your attitude toward them changed?
- Is there a new person in either of your parents' life?

- How do you feel about it?
- What changes has this caused for you and the rest of the family?
- How does your other parent behave and talk about it?
- How does the new person treat you?
- If the new person has children, how do you feel about them?
- How do they treat you?
- What are you doing to help you feel good about yourself and to give you a feeling of control over your situation?
- Do you have someone to talk to about what's happening and how you're feeling?

One More River to Cross

It's Saturday night and the friends have arrived at Jan's house.

"I can't believe how long it's been since we were all together," Jan says to Neil.

"I know," he says. "I guess with people going away to college, people staying here at school or working, different vacations and everything, we're all over the place."

"One thing all of us are doing the same is looking for jobs and trying to figure out what we want to do with the rest of our lives," Jamie says.

"Some of us," says Ben, "are trying to figure out what our parents are going to do with the rest of theirs!"

Liz laughs and says, "Yeah, it's hard to make my own plans when I'm not sure what Mom and Dad are going to do."

"Well," Dana says, "I finally decided that, one way or the other, if I've got a job, it makes it a lot less of a big deal what Mom's doing or decides to do. And it makes me feel a whole lot better toward her and about myself."

"I know what you mean," says Jamie. "As long as I was waiting around to see what was going to happen next, I was getting angrier and angrier at both my parents. I don't understand why, exactly, but maybe it was because I felt out of control of my own life and I kept waiting for them to bail me out."

"Yeah, I felt that way, too," Liz says. "Ben, you helped me a lot with that. You helped me see that I was angry at them for breaking up the family and making it so that I couldn't count on the way things used to be, or count on them to do what parents are 'supposed' to do—whatever that is. Instead, now that I count on myself to make what I want happen, I can accept what's happening with the family a lot better. At 19, I guess it's time, anyway, to start taking responsibility for my own life even if my parents weren't getting a divorce."

"I guess parents' getting a divorce can be a real motivator," Jamie says with a laugh. "Clarke, you've always had a job and seemed independent even without your parents' getting a divorce. What's the secret?"

"I'm not really sure," Clarke answers. "I guess with two older brothers making work look like fun and not having to go to Mom and Dad all the time to ask for money, I couldn't wait to get a job. Mom and Dad certainly never discouraged the idea, either. Listening to everyone makes me realize that, no matter what's going on at home, all of us are at the point when we don't want to have to depend on the family so much, and we want to be more on our own. Oh, hi, Kate. You made it."

"How was the 'gathering'?" asks Dana.

"Oh, it was OK, a lot better that I thought it would be," answers Kate. "Actually, Dave—that's my mother's boyfriend—is really a good guy, and his kids aren't so bad, either. They're just so young. Just before we left for the restaurant, Dad showed up. That was a little tense. Thank God, it didn't get unpleasant. Sometimes I think this whole thing would be easier if Mom and Dad weren't right in the same town, if Dad lived farther away."

"I don't know," Dana says. "Dad moved away as soon as he and Mom separated, and I miss him a lot. It seems to take longer for them to work things out, because they're not around each other and have to give things more time to get resolved. And I really miss sharing with him what I'm doing and having him around just to talk to and do things with."

"I guess you're right," Kate says. "I suppose there's something good and bad in everything. So, what have I missed? Has anyone won the lottery or solved all the world's problems yet?"

"No," Jan laughs, "we've just been sitting around talking about how we're all ready to leave the nest—fly the coop, as the saying goes. It's so good getting back together again."

"Yeah," Neil says, "it feels great to be able to just talk about what's on our minds and listen to what's happening with everyone."

"We figured one thing out," Ben says. "With or without divorcing parents, all of us have some rivers to cross, and I'm pretty excited thinking about it and seeing what all of us end up doing. You know, all this talk is making me real hungry. Anybody bring any food?"

Questions

- Do both of your parents live in the same town?
- Do you live with one of your parents?
- Do you have a chance to talk to and visit your other parent as much as you'd like?
- If one of your parents does live far away, how does that make you feel?
- Do you still have a good relationship with that parent? How do you stay in touch and schedule time to be together?

- If you don't have a good relationship with one of your parents, what do you think is standing in the way?
- Do you think both you and your parents have an equal responsibility to work on building a new relationship?
- If you live with neither of your parents, what do you do to maintain your relationship with them and your bothers and sisters?
- What do they do to maintain their relationship with you?
- What are some good results of your parents getting a divorce?
- At age 18 or 19, do you think it's time to start being more independent, with or without a divorce?

Thinking back over all the stories you just read, answer the following questions.

- Which issues in the stories are ones that you are dealing with?
- What other issues upset you?
- Describe how each of the situations you're dealing with makes you feel.
- What have you done about these issues so far?
- Which feelings expressed by the young people in the stories have you felt?
- What other feelings are bothering you?
- Whom can you talk to about these things?
- Whom do you feel closest to in your family?

Crossing the Rivers One at a Time

The 18- and 19-year-olds in the stories you've been reading stand at a unique juncture in their lives, just as you do. You, like them, have battled through your teenage years and have arrived at the transition between adolescence and adulthood. You are ready to loosen your grip on your family as you move out on your own. Whether you are out working, at college in your hometown, or far away from home, you are separating from your family emotionally and becoming more confident about being physically separated from them as well.

The confusion that exists in your family because of the divorce takes away the solid foundation you have always counted on. It's natural to ask, "Why now?" and "Why me?" as well as to feel angry, sad, and disappointed about what is happening. But this doesn't change the fact that you are at the point in your life to face forward and move ahead. Your circumstances at home may accelerate your need to develop some financial independence and may also force you to take a more active role in and responsibility for planning your immediate future. Again, you would normally be doing this now anyway, with or without a divorce.

The divorce is a crisis that has happened in your family, but it is a divorce between your mother and father. You were not responsible for making it happen, but you are responsible for what you want to make happen in your own life. How you handle this crisis will determine how you deal with other ones that are bound to occur in your life. You can meet the crisis, make the necessary adjustments, and move on, or you can bog down emotionally and become permanently stuck in a defeatist, "I'm the victim" mind-set.

The structure of your family is changing just as you are changing. Certain things will not change. You have, and will continue to have, the love of your parents, whether or not they always appear to be actively involved in your life.

You are at the brink of the second decade of your life. Physically, mentally, and emotionally, you are prepared to enter it. You have every reason to expect a successful and happy adulthood—not because of circumstances outside of yourself, but because of what *you* choose to do to make it that way.

Questions

- What purpose does your family serve for you?
- What are your family's traits that you're proud of? that you're not proud of?
- Where do you find your strength?
- What do you think are your strengths?
- What kinds of people do you see yourself with?
- What are some of your life goals?
- Where do you see yourself in five years?

Summary

Main Focuses

- Your uncertainty about where to go from here, what role your family is going to play, and how the divorce will affect you and your plans: Can I afford to go to college? How can I get a job? Do my parents love me? Where will I live? Whom can I turn to when I need help? Do I have what it takes to make it?
- The effect on you of:
  - — Parental warfare
  - — The absence of one or both parents in your life

— Your feelings of loyalty for both of your parents

— Your feelings of responsibility for your parents' emotional burdens

— Your parents' new relationships

Self-Esteem Exercises

- Make a list of the things you do well.
- Make a list of the people you really enjoy being with. What do you like about them? Are these qualities that you want to develop in yourself? What do these people like about you? Are these qualities you're proud of?
- Make a list of three things you've done lately that you're proud of.
- Make a list of three things you would like to learn how to do that would benefit you and others.
- Name some people who can help you start to learn about these three things.
- Describe your ideal job. Name the skills you have that make you suitable for the job. Name the skills you need to develop or learn to be suitable for the job.
- Make a list of activities that help you let off steam safely.
- Make a list of the people and things that matter the most to you, and devote time to them. Make sure you don't get so busy that you forget to make time for them and for yourself.
- Give yourself credit for doing the best you can with your circumstances and carrying out your first obligation: **Taking responsibility for yourself and making your life what you want it to be.**

Part Three

Developmental Stages and Divorce for Ages 20 and Up

Chapter 7
Early Adulthood
(AGES 20–29)

"Men at Work"
—AUSTRALIAN ROCK GROUP

Instructions

This chapter is written just for you and people your age whose parents are going through a divorce. By pinpointing the very special issues that concern your age group when confronted by a divorce, the material in the chapter will help you move smoothly through this experience with no lasting ill effects.

Most of the chapter is made up of episodes about a family going through a divorce. The people in the family are facing the same feelings and issues you are. At the end of each episode and throughout the chapter, there are questions for you to answer that will make the material more meaningful for you. Your answers will give you information about yourself and the situation that will help you put this experience in perspective. This new perspective will make it possible for you to work through this experience and successfully come to terms with the divorce and the new family structure. Use a separate sheet of paper for your answers.

You may want to share this chapter with someone whose advice you trust, or you may want to read and work on it by yourself. You choose what works best for you.

"Choose a Job You Love and You Will Never Work for a Living" – Confucius

"Lara? It's Jay. I called in for messages and you got a call-back from the firm you interviewed with last week, and your mom called too."

"Thanks, Jay," Lara says. "I can't believe it! That was the job I was really interested in. Wouldn't it be great to be *permanently* employed and out of this temp stuff? Now I'm nervous. Oh, I want that job so bad. It's just what I described in my 'ideal job' exercise. I'm so excited I didn't even ask you how your meeting went."

"It went fine," Jay says. "We got our assignments for the next month. It looks like I'll be on the road most of next week. When they said this was an accelerated training program, they weren't kidding."

"I'll miss you," Lara says, "but this sure is the best experience you could have if you do decide to go to graduate school. I'll go by the market on the way home and pick up something for dinner."

"OK," says Jay, "I'll pick up a video after work. Listen, if it gets late, forget the market. We can order pizza."

"Hey, we're really getting this division of labor down since we moved in together," Lara laughs.

"At work they'd call it 'economic efficiency,'" Jay chuckles.

"You know, this is Mom's first call," Lara says. "Maybe she's getting used to the idea of our 'new arrangement.' Don't work too hard."

"Around here that's unavoidable," Jay says. "See you tonight."

"OK. Thanks for the messages."

Questions

- What are your living arrangements? Do you live with your parents? alone? with a roommate of the same sex or of the opposite sex?
- Are you financially independent of your parents?
- Do you have a "significant other"?
- Are you married? single?
- Are you at school? Do you work, as well?
- Do you work full-time?
- Do you have a strong support group at school? at work? outside school and work?
- Do you feel strongly attached to your family?
- Are most of your activities outside of school or work spent with family members?
- Is most of your time outside of school or work spent with people other than your family?
- Do you feel emotionally independent of your family?
- Do you feel responsible for your family?

Working It Out

"Hi, Mom. It's Lara. Jay said you called."

"Hello, Darling," Mom says. "I'm so glad you called. I've been thinking, you and Jay and this living arrangement..."

Lara cuts in, "Mom, don't start. Jay and I have made this decision. We're happy with it and it's our business. Is this why you called? If it is, I've got a lot of work to do. I'll see you next week."

"Lara," Mom says, "I'm sorry. I know I promised not to talk about it anymore. I'm just so upset I don't know what I'm saying. You're the first one I've called."

Lara interrupts again. "Mom, what is it? What's happened?"

Mom says, "It's your father. He wants a divorce."

"What!" Lara shrieks. "He what? When did this happen?"

Mom says, "This morning at breakfast. I just don't know where to turn. I feel absolutely turned inside out."

"Mom," Lara says, "how did this happen? I never noticed anything. You seemed just the same as always."

"That's what I thought, too, at first when he told me," Mom says. "But I've been thinking about it all morning since he left. I guess we've been drifting apart for a long time. Your father working, me running the house. We never really put time aside for us. When there was a little time, there always seemed to be something else more important that we needed to do. When we talked, it was always something to do with money, the household, you children, his job—never just about the two of us. We got out of the habit of anything that was just us. I don't know. When the last of you kids went off to college, there didn't seem to be much for us to talk about. I thought it would gradually take care of itself, but it really hasn't. The fun we've had has been when one of you has come back and we've all gotten together. Otherwise, we've just seemed to go our separate ways. I knew that was the way it was. I can see all that now, but I never thought this would happen. Never. Never. I just don't know what to hold on to, what to do."

"Oh, Mom," Lara says, "that's so sad. I had no idea. I guess I just thought you'd always be there, the two of you. I never really thought about it. Mom, is there something I can do? Do you want me to come over?"

"No," Mom answers, "I still have to call Tyler. Will's going to be in town on business, so I can tell him tonight. He'll have to tell Renee when he goes home. I just can't stand the thought of telling her. When she married Will, we really became her family since her parents died. Now she's lost this family, too, in a way. I'm sorry I had to tell you like this, but I didn't know any other way to do it. You'll always be our little girl, no matter what."

"Mom, there's no other way to tell something like this," Lara says. "Please don't worry about it. You've got enough on your mind. After all, I should have a lot of practice. Most of my friends have gone through this. I'll come by after work, OK?"

"I'd love that, Darling," Mom answers. "I'll see you then."

Questions

- How did you first hear that your parents were getting a divorce?
- What was your initial reaction?
- In the conversation when you first learned about the divorce, was the person who told you taking care of you, or did you feel you were taking care of that person, or did you feel you were both taking care of each other?
- How did your parents behave emotionally when you first spoke to them about the divorce?
- Did you feel you wanted to take sides between your parents?
- Had you noticed problems in your parents' relationship, or were you surprised?

- Do you feel you have to support your mother emotionally? your father?
- How do you think the divorce will affect your life?
- What changes do you think you will have to make?

Working It Through

"Lara, how'd it go?" Jay asks.

"Oh, Jay," says Lara. "Poor Mom. She doesn't know what's hit her. I'm really glad I went by to see her. It gave us a chance to hold each other and cry it out. I guess there's going to be a lot more of that. You know, you can already feel Dad's not there anymore. All the little things that remind me of him are gone—his briefcase, the smell of his pipe smoke, his jacket on the back of the chair, the sound of the TV on some sports channel. It's got to be awful for Mom. Whether they had a lot to say to each other or not, at least they were there for each other: a schedule, a routine. Now it feels empty. And Mom just sits there, staring around. She'd start to say something and then she'd just look off, seeing something or hearing something in her own mind."

"It seems awfully fast," Jay says. "Your father getting all his stuff. It only happened this morning. Your mother is so lucky having you nearby. Imagine if all of you lived out of town. At least she isn't alone. If she needs something, you or I can be there in minutes."

"Yeah," Lara says, "it's good for me, too, if I need her. I didn't realize how hard this hit me. I talked to Dad before I left work. I thought maybe it was something they could talk out, and once they really thought about it, they'd get back together and things would be like they'd always been, except better. That's not going to happen. Dad is real final about this. He's talked to Mom, and this weekend he's going to take the rest of his personal stuff. He has a furnished apartment until he can find one he can move all his things into. It's going to be strange to go to the home I pretty much grew up in and see it all picked apart. It's going to be terrible for Mom. Dad does seem to moving awfully fast. I guess he's been thinking about this for a while. It's probably best to get this first part over with as quickly as possible and not drag it out. If something's going to happen anyway, I'd want to get it over with, not wake up each morning wondering when the ax is going to fall, prolonging the agony. Maybe we could ask Mom if she wants to stay with us overnight while Dad is moving his things out."

"Where would she sleep?" Jay asks. "On the sofa? I don't know. Things are a little tense between her and me, right now. Anyway, I'm not so sure that's such a good idea. So much is changing for her already. It might really be better for her to at least be in her own surroundings, where things are familiar. She can be alone when she wants to be and not feel like she's got to perform. I remember when my parents got divorced. I never knew when to be around and when not to be around. Also, you've been thinking so much about your mom and dad, you haven't really had a chance for it to sink in for you."

"Oh, Jay," Lara says, "what in the world would I do if you weren't here? I guess I'm talking and thinking so much about them so that I won't have to really look at what it all means for me and how I feel. You know, it's like the floor has just caved in under me and the ceiling has just collapsed on my head. I've always felt so independent, but I always thought my family would be just the way it's always been. Will, Tyler, and I would go out into the world. Sure, we'd go through some changes, but Mom and Dad would always be the same. You know, I miss Dad already. He'll be around somewhere, but it's going to be so different. Before, I could drop by, catch up with them, tell them what I was doing—kill two birds with one stone. Now, it won't be so easy. See Mom one day, see Dad the next, if I can catch him. Two phone calls, instead of one. Take care of Mom. Take care of Dad. They're supposed to take care of each other.

Maybe have Mom move in with us. I wonder if I should move back home until she gets on her feet…"

"Hey, hold it," Jay says. "Slow down. Take it one step at a time. Your parents are the same people they were yesterday. Just because they're getting a divorce doesn't mean you have to start running a convalescent home. All of you are going to be all right. Your parents are just going to have a 'new arrangement' that takes some getting used to, just like we have a 'new arrangement.'"

"Yeah," Lara says, "except our 'new arrangement' brought two people together. Theirs is splitting two apart and changing it for all of us. I guess you're right, though, when you really look at it. It's just changes and getting used to the changes and how they're going to affect all of us. Well, at least for now, our 'new arrangement' won't be the burning topic of family discussions."

"With all this going on," Jay says, "I forgot to ask you about your call-back."

"Oh, I forgot, too," says Lara. "I did have a chance to call them. It looks like they're as excited about me as I am about them. We've set up a final interview for tomorrow. Unless something really comes off the tracks, I think I've got it. Isn't that great? Yesterday, I was a temp worker with a permanent family. Today, it looks like I've got a future as a permanent worker with a temporary family. What a roller coaster!"

"Hey," Jay says, "you've still got a permanent family. It's just going through some temporary adjustments until it's in its new, permanent arrangement!"

"Jay, you're wonderful. Thanks for trying to cheer me up. I'm exhausted just thinking about it," Lara says. "Let's order the pizza. I'm starved. Then I'm going to call Mom and see how she's doing. I'm sure glad Will's in town."

Questions

- How soon after the divorce decision did one of your parents move out?
- Do you feel you have to take care of one or both of your parents?
- Do you think about your parents' getting back together? Is that realistic to expect?
- Do you feel you will lose touch with one or both of your parents?
- How does that make you feel? Is there something you can do about that?
- Will either of your parents look to you for emotional or financial support?
- How do you feel about that?
- If you are living away from your parents, do you feel you should move back in with one of them or have one of them move in with you?
- How does that make you feel?
- Would either of those choices make sense in terms of your life and what you are trying to do?

A Piece of Work

"Oh, Will," Renee says, "I didn't realize you were on the phone. I'm sorry I was making so much noise in the kitchen."

"I didn't even notice," Will says. "That was Dad on the phone. You know, it's the first time I've talked to him since this whole thing started. Poor Mom. Wait till she hears this."

"What?" Renee asks. "What's happened now?"

"Not 'now,'" answers Will, "but apparently for some time already. I was so angry at him when he told me, it was all I could do not to slam the phone down. You know the associate of his we met last summer when Dad was in town? The one we had dinner with, that you liked so much?"

"The divorced woman with two children?" Renee asks. "She was impressive, great looking, too, with all those credentials. She made me think it's possible to have a real career and be a woman as well."

"Yeah, she's the one," Will says. "Impressive? Maybe 'pressing' is more like it. She 'pressed' herself right into Dad's life. According to Dad, they were just business associates, and then 'one thing led to another and the next thing we knew we were in love.' In love! What is he talking about? What about Mom? Is she just an old rag? What about us? What about the family? Yeah, some business associate. Anyway, he says they really tried to fight it, didn't see each other, that he even suggested counseling to Mom to try to 'bring their relationship back to life.' Like it was a corpse or something. He said none of it worked. He said he just wanted to be with this woman for the rest of his life, that she's the best thing that's ever happened to him. He's telling this to me, his son! Is he crazy? He says he wants us to get to know her and we'll see why he feels the way he does. I couldn't believe I was hearing this, that this person babbling all this stuff was my father, the man I've always looked up to, the person who taught me what it meant to be a man, have integrity, be responsible. This is really going to rip it for Tyler and Lara, not to mention Mom. He is really a piece of work! He even wanted me to tell them. Can you believe it? I said, 'Not on your life! This is your Fourth of July show. It can blow up in your face, not mine.' That got his attention. He said he'd call them later this evening. I almost asked why he didn't have Miss Business Associate cover the assignment for him since she's handling everything else, but I didn't. Then he asked when you and I could get together with him and her. That was too much. I just said, 'Later, Dad,' and hung up. I'm 29. I've always thought I could handle pretty much anything, but this pushed me right over the edge. I don't know if I'll ever think of him the same way."

"Oh, Will," Renee says. "How horrible for you. With a divorce, sooner or later, both your parents were bound to meet someone, if they were lucky. I'm so sorry it had to happen this way for all of you, including your Dad. You know, he's a good man. I'm sure he didn't want this to happen. From what you told me your Mom said, they really haven't had a relationship for a long time. I would hate to live like that. The divorce, for all the losses and changes it will cause, is probably a good thing for both of them in the long run, but your Dad's new relationship is just going to make what's hard to begin with even harder."

"I guess you're right," Will says. "I'm afraid I can't be very objective right now. It's going to take me a while to get over being angry at him, for the divorce and now for this other thing. I know both Mom and Dad had a part in letting their relationship go, but it just seems like Mom is left with fewer options."

"That's probably true, for now," Renee says. "But this whole experience may get your Mom off on a new foot. She may just bloom and get out there and do something on her own and for herself."

"Maybe so," Will says. "But right now she's going to need a lot of support. Renee, I feel bad about this, but we're going to have to postpone our plans for this weekend. I'm going to go back down to Mom's tomorrow. I think we need to be all together to go over this and help each other deal with it. I can't see doing it over the phone. I don't expect you to go with me. I know it's going to be unpleasant, but it would sure mean a lot to me if you could be there."

"Oh, Will," Renee says, "I wouldn't think of being anywhere else! I can get a few days off from work. I'm overdue and it's a slow time now, anyway, so I can stay with your Mom after you leave if it looks like that would help. One thing, though: Right now, all of us need to help each other, including your dad, but it won't be good for any of us if we start living each other's lives. We won't help anyone by hovering over them. The sooner we can get all of us adjusted to the new circumstances and get on with our lives, the better off we'll all be. Your mom and dad are good people, and all of you have been wonderful to me. This is still a great family to be a part of."

"Renee, no wonder you're so special to me," Will says. "All of a sudden I feel fifty pounds lighter. I really had it going there—me holding up the world, the whole family stapled on my back, staggering forward under the burden. I'd forgotten I really do have a wonderful family and each of us is more independent than the next. I guess Mom, Dad, Tyler, and Lara want their own lives just as much as we do. We're lucky we have all of us to share the burden. I'm sure glad I'm not in Dad's shoes. I know this can't be easy for him. I'd better call Mom and let her know we're coming."

"OK," Renee says. "Give her my love. I'll go and start packing."

Questions

- How do you feel about your mother and father having a relationship with a new person?
- Does it make you feel protective toward the other parent?
- Do you feel pulled between getting to know the new person, accepting him or her into your life, and your loyalty toward the parent that person is replacing?
- Was there a new person in your parent's life before the divorce?
- How do you feel about that?

- Do you feel both your parents contributed to the breakdown of their relationship?
- How have your parents treated each other since the divorce?
- How have your parents treated you since the divorce?
- Describe your parents' relationship before the divorce.
- Was it the kind of relationship you'd want to have?
- Describe your ideal relationship.

Working Through It

"Tyler, oh, I'm so glad I got you," Lara says. "I've been trying for two days. Are you all right?"

"Lara," Tyler answers, "have you gotten my messages? I've been trying to reach you and Will ever since Mom called. I can't believe this. Did you have any idea? I really feel cut off from all of you. Do you think I should come home or something?"

"Tyler, that's why I really wanted to talk to you," says Lara. "Will just called to tell me that he and Renee are coming down this weekend so that all of us can get together. Can you get home, or do you want me to come get you?"

"Aw, Lara, you still think I'm your helpless little brother," Tyler says. "Thanks, Big Sis. I'm overdue being home. I'll find a ride or something, but I'll be there. How's Mom? Are you OK? Ever since Mom called, I've been doing a lot of thinking about all of us. I hadn't realized just how much I'd been living in my own little world. Do you think we could have made it better for them? They always put us first, and I, for one, never wanted it any other way. Now I think maybe we helped create the mess."

"Tyler, sure, you're right," Lara says. "Mom lived and breathed us twenty-four hours a day and, yeah, Dad has always worked really hard to support all of us. But not for a minute is this our fault. There wasn't anything we were going to do that would have changed what's happened. Their relationship, whether it worked or not, was between the two of them. What we can do now is help each other work through this. It's funny how good things come out of the worst situations. It's been a long time since we've all gotten together."

"Yeah, I guess," says Tyler. "There's something else I want to ask you about that I didn't want to bother Mom with. She has so much on her mind. Do you think this is going to mess up my staying in school? I feel bad bringing it up, thinking about myself when I should be thinking about Mom and Dad and all of you. I guess what I'm trying to say is, what's the money situation going to be like? Do you know?"

"No, I don't," answers Lara. "No one's really focused on things like that yet. Everyone's just been trying to deal with the suddenness of all of this and the feelings. I don't think the money thing will be a problem where this school year is concerned. You've always had a job, so that will be the same. If things get tight for graduate school, you may have to take out a student loan, but don't start worrying about that before there's reason to. You really should bring it up when we're all together. I think there are going to be a lot of questions like that. All of us need to know what to expect, so that we can make plans. Tyler, don't feel bad bringing that up. At least you're being practical, instead of just wallowing around in feelings. Whoops, there goes my 'call waiting.' See you tomorrow night."

"OK," says Tyler, "I'm glad we've talked. Say 'Hi' to Jay."

Questions

- When you first heard about the divorce, what questions did you have about how it would affect your plans?
- Is there someone you can talk to about your concerns?

- Do you worry about burdening your parent(s) with these questions?
- Do you feel, somehow, that it's your fault that your parents are getting a divorce?
- Is there someone you respect and trust that you can talk to, to help you understand that the breakup is not your responsibility but is between your parents?

Working Together

"All right, all right," Mom says, "I know you're all upset with your father, but I think all of us need to give that some thought. Is it because of the divorce or is it because of Kim? Is it because you're concerned about me, or is it because you're thinking about what you've lost and how all this will affect you? No, don't answer right now. Take a minute to go over what I've just said. These are all things we need to think about, so that we can deal with everything that's happened and that's going to happen. I've had a lot of time to think about all of this. My heart breaks for all of us, including your father. I know we have lost the picture that all of us have been very comfortable with for a long time. That picture has many pieces and parts. Some of the pieces go way, way back, before any of you were born. Your father and I shared young dreams and made many promises to the future, just like each of you is doing now. Pieces of that picture are Christmases and Thanksgivings, celebrations that we won't share all together as we used to. The part of the picture that was the old familiar shoe isn't there to find comfort in anymore. Much is lost that can't come again. It's natural to feel angry about those losses and very sad that so much has changed. No one wanted this to happen, certainly not your father. He's lost the same things we have."

"Mom," Tyler says, "it's all I've been thinking about since you first called, all the times together as a family. Maybe I'm way out of line saying this, but Lara and Will have had a lot more of those times than I have. What I want to know is, can we all be together at my graduation? It's coming up in only six weeks. Or is that another piece of the picture that I've lost? Everyone's talked about how angry they are at Dad. For me, sure, I wish this whole thing hadn't happened and that I'd never laid eyes on Kim, but I've worked hard to get through college and to make good grades, and I really want all of you to be at my graduation, Dad included. If getting Dad there means having Kim too, then yes, Kim too. I know we're talking about the picture and all the pieces and parts, but just for that moment, on that day, I want all of my family there, together with me, and then after that we can go back to the parts and the pieces and the picture."

"Tyler," Mom says, "of course we'll be at your graduation. I can speak for your father, as well. He'd be there no matter what. Your graduation is a landmark in your life, and none of us would miss it. We've had many landmarks like this and will have many more. The divorce doesn't change that. All it means is that we'll come to these occasions, these special moments in each of our lives, through different doors, but with no less love and pride. We may not all live under the same roof—we haven't done that for some time—but we are a part of each other's lives and always will be. That will never change. Your father and I are bound together by the past we've shared, and we will share part of our future together through you. As others come into our lives, as Renee and Jay have, we'll welcome them and enrich and be enriched, in return. The picture we've known so well isn't really lost or gone, but it has changed and we have to recognize that and get used to it. It will be a whole lot easier to handle all of this once you understand that. I, for one, am looking forward to all the new parts and pieces, whatever they may be. I can't believe that only last week the most crucial things on my mind were whether or not I'd be able to find a replacement for the fabric on the living room sofa and whether Lara and Jay were wise to move in together."

"Jay," Lara says, "things must be returning to normal if Mom's talking about us again. Mom, all this time I've been so concerned about you, that you were going to fall apart or something. Meanwhile, I'm the one who's been a wreck. I don't know about everyone else, but this whole thing has reminded me of how precious all of you are to me. I was a little nervous at first about both Jay and me being here, but now I'm so glad he talked me into both of us coming. Tyler, your graduation's going to be the best. We'll all be there, as Mom said, 'through different doors,' but there nonetheless. We're not about to let you go up on that stage without a few catcalls to keep you loose."

"Speaking for Renee and me," Will says, "as bad as the last few days have been, it's reminded us just how important everyone in this family is to us. That includes Kim, too, if she's going to be a part of Dad's life now. We've been so busy keeping up with our jobs and being with our friends up there, I hadn't realized how out of touch we'd become. It's going to be hard getting used to 'the new picture,' but if it means spending more time on the phone or visits back and forth, great. When this whole thing started, I thought, 'Oh, terrific. This is just what I need. I don't have enough time as it is. How am I going to deal with this too, not to mention being overwhelmed by the whole idea of you and Dad getting a divorce and the family coming apart?' Mom, I don't know how you can be so calm about all of this. Why aren't you angry and yelling? It just doesn't seem real to me, the way you're handling it."

"Will, I have been angry, very angry, but that was between your father and me. I think we've always done a good job as parents, and maybe what makes me proudest of all is that we never let our anger, or whatever, with each other affect any of you. What I have felt and still feel is a great sadness about so many things. It will take me a long time to let go of that, but I'm going to make it a point to spend as little time as possible thinking about it. What's to be gained by dwelling on something that's over and done with? I can't afford the luxury of those negative thoughts. I want to get on with my life, and I want all of you to do the same. I don't want to see any long faces around here. That won't help anybody. I want to enjoy what all of you are doing, but I'm also really looking forward to trying out some new things for myself."

"Mom," Lara says, "we're the ones who're supposed to be unpredictable. Instead, first Dad, now you, are a surprise-a-minute. I can't afford to feel sorry for myself about all this or be emotionally traumatized, or I'll miss what happens next. My new job doesn't sound like headline news after all this!"

"What you've said, Mom," Tyler says, "means to me that each of us has a lot to deal with and a lot to get used to, I guess—each in our own way. I know I felt so angry and scared when you first called and, yeah, sad, too, but this is the way it is, so we might as well make the best of it. Now that we've all had a chance to talk about it and get some of our feelings out, it really doesn't seem so bad after all. I just want to know that all of you will be there if I need to be reminded."

"Tyler, you've said it much better than I did," Mom says. "All of you have helped me so much just by being here. We've gotten over the hardest part, but we're all going to need to help each other get through the rest of this."

"I'm sure glad to hear that," Will laughs. "Short of one of us being run over by a Mack truck, I can't imagine what more we could have crammed into this week."

"Maybe we'd better call Dad," Lara chuckles, "and tell him to stay out of traffic. Mom, I guess Jay and I'd better get going. Tomorrow's an early one for both of us."

"I'm glad we all got together and talked this out," Tyler says. "I feel a lot better about everything. I think I'll call Dad and see how he's doing."

Questions and Exercises

- Make a list of the losses and changes the divorce will cause for you.
- Have you had a chance to sit down and talk to the members of your family about the divorce?
- Have you talked to them about your feelings? Have they talked to you about theirs?
- How is each of you acting? Angry? Confused? Sad? Scared? List other feelings.
- Are there bad feelings toward one particular person?
- Do you feel the divorce will make your relationships with your brothers and sisters closer? Which ones, and why?
- Do you feel it will make your relationship with one or both of your parents closer? Which one, and why?
- Do you feel it will make these relationships less close? Which ones, and why?
- Have you thought about and discussed how family occasions will be handled in the future?
- If members of your family are having trouble handling the divorce, can you help them?
- If you're having trouble handling the divorce, is there someone who can help you?
- How do you think the divorce will affect your life outside of the family?
- How do you think it will affect your relationships outside of the family?

Thinking about all the episodes you've just read, answer the following questions:

- How does the family in the chapter compare with yours? What's similar? What's different?
- Whom did you identify with the most, and why? the least, and why?
- Which issues are ones you are dealing with?
  - — Parents' emotional needs
  - — Siblings' emotional needs
  - — The effect of the divorce on your independence
  - — The effect of the divorce on you financially
  - — Divided loyalty between parents
  - — Your feeling of responsibility for the divorce
  - — Disillusionment with your parent(s)
  - — Your parent(s)' new relationship
  - — Other issues
- Describe how each of these issues makes you feel.
- Whom can you talk to about these issues and your feelings?

Working It All Out

Your age group covers a broad spectrum. Some of you are just starting your career or finishing your education, and still live with your family. Others of you have moved away from your immediate family, are further along with your career, have a home of your own, and, in some cases, have started a family. Whether the divorce explodes right on top of you or you feel the explosion at a distance, the effect is devastating.

With or without a divorce, all of you in this age group share the feeling of being pulled between pursuing your own life, independent of your original family, and limiting your independence to serve the needs of that family. It is during your 20s that you learn to strike the balance to meet both of these needs.

Divorce brings a new dimension to this tug of war. It complicates an already complicated situation. Ordinarily, you wouldn't hesitate to move to another town if a job opportunity presented itself. Now, your concern for your family might make you think twice about it. As a member of that family, you do share responsibility for its welfare, but it's important for you to remember, even in the midst of this crisis, that you are responsible for taking care of your own life and well-being, as well.

You are not responsible for your parents' divorce, but you are implicated in it, anyway, whether you are still living at home or have moved away. The effect of the divorce is a challenge both for you personally and for your family as a whole to work out. As a young adult, you are capable of making a real contribution to help yourself and the others meet this challenge, respond to the demands of the crisis, and prepare for the new family structure that evolves after the dust settles.

As difficult and emotionally trying as this time is for you, it also presents you with rewarding opportunities. It gives you the chance to learn how to master the events in your life, instead of being victimized by them, to discover strengths in yourself and others, and to find new sources of support that you weren't aware of. Confronting and successfully working through the issues that come out of this experience will affect your view of yourself and your family members. The resolution of these issues will also mean that you won't carry over unwanted baggage into your present and future relationships outside of the family. You will restrict the outcome of your parents' marriage to the nature of the two of them and their relationship and know that you have every reason to expect to have fulfilling and enduring relationships of your own. Most important, it will mean that the divorce will have no lasting destructive effect on you. Your life is yours to make of it what you choose.

Questions

- What will be your role in helping the family deal with the divorce?
- Who do you think will have the hardest time with the divorce?
- Who is in the best position to help them?
- Who will help you deal with the divorce? who inside the family? who outside of the family?
- How will the needs of the family interfere with your usual schedule?

Summary

Main Focuses

- The emotional effect on you of your parents' divorce: fear, anger, worry, sadness, disillusionment, guilt
- The line between your helping your parents with their needs and your need to continue to develop yourself as an independent entity
- The ability to see the difference between what has happened to your parents' relationship and what you want to make of your life and your relationships
- The ability to look at your parents and their relationship with objectivity and compassion
- The ability to take control of your feelings, needs, and life, rather than letting the crisis dictate your behavior and emotions

Common Concerns

- Parental warfare
- The absence of one or both parents in your life
- Your feelings of loyalty for both of your parents
- Your feelings of responsibility for your parents' emotional burdens
- Your parents' new relationships

Self-Esteem Exercises

- Make a list of what things you're afraid the divorce will cause. Which ones are reasonable fears and which aren't? What can you do about the reasonable ones?
- Decide how you can sensibly help your parents and the other family members with the divorce.
- Make a list of your feelings about your parents and the divorce.
- Give yourself permission to have these feelings and to understand that they are a natural response to the losses and changes that are happening because of your parents' decision.
- Recognize that their decision and the divorce are not your fault.
- Decide to start letting go of your negative feelings so that they can't become destructive to you, your plans, and your relationships.
- Keep in mind that the divorce is an event that has happened in your life but that you have the power to control how it will affect you, long term.

- Make a list of happy memories that you have of your family before the divorce.
- Make a list of ways to create happy memories with the family as it now is.
- Remember, as important as this experience is, it is not important enough to permanently interrupt your life. **As soon as you can, come to terms with it and get on with your own life.**

Chapter 8
Adulthood
(AGE 30 AND UP)

"Don't Worry 'Bout a Thing"
—FROM "THREE LITTLE BIRDS" BY BOB MARLEY

Instructions

The broad responsibilities and obligations of your age group make the divorce of your parents at this point in your life particularly difficult and complicated. This chapter is written for you with this in mind. It is designed to help you recognize and work through the very special issues that affect you and that will come up for you during this time, so that you can avoid long-term ill effects.

The chapter sets up a fictional family that is going through just what you are. In each episode, the issues and feelings you are experiencing are pinpointed and expressed by the family members. There are questions after each episode to help you make the material more personal and meaningful for you. The rest of the chapter includes additional information and questions to further aid you in handling this experience successfully, coming to terms with it yourself, and helping you deal with the needs of your parents, your siblings, and your own children. Use a separate sheet for your answers.

You may want to share this chapter with someone, or you may want to read and work on it by yourself. You decide what works best for you.

What's to Worry?

BEEP: "Debbie, it's Mary. Sure, that's fine. I can do carpool for you next week while you're away on the business trip."

BEEP: "Mom, if you get this message before noon, can you bring me my glove for practice, on your way back to work?"

BEEP: "Hi, Deb, it's Sally. Can you and Kirk come for dinner Saturday?"

BEEP: "Kirk, I missed you at the office. It looks like a late night again. Can you cover dinner? Todd should be home from practice by six-thirty, and Hillary has play practice until seven. Don't forget to give Pacer his heartworm pill. I'll be home as soon as I can. See you then, Darling. Bye."

BEEP: "Deb and Kirk, it's Grandma. Give me a call when you have a chance. We'd love to stay with Hillary and Todd while you're gone. It's great you're in the same business so that you can go on these trips together."

Questions and Exercises

- Write down a typical weekday and weekend day schedule, including meals; errands; job; time with the children, friends, and other family members; chores; showers; dressing; commuting; leisure activities; and so on.
- Next, rank their importance in terms of time allocation.
- Next, rank their emotional importance to you.
- Notice which ones can preempt others if there is a time crunch or if an additional demand is placed on you.
- Where do your emotional needs rank?

What, Me Worry?

"Dad," Hillary asks, "do Grandma and Grandpa have to stay with us while you're at the conference? After all, we're 15 and 13. We should be old enough to take care of ourselves. They're even stricter than you and Mom."

"Yeah, I know," Dad laughs. "Are we ruining your plans for an all-night party?"

"Dad, not tuna casserole again," says Todd. "I'm beginning to grow gills. I'm sure glad Grandma and Grandpa are coming. We'll finally get some decent food around here. She's the best cook in the world. Hillary, why are you glaring at me? You didn't really think you'd talk Dad and Mom into letting us stay by ourselves, did you? You may be happy with microwave miracles, but I'm a growing boy and I need good food. I can't wait for Grandma's blueberry muffins!"

"Well, at least," says Hillary, "can Grandpa give me some driving practice?"

"Oh, now I see," Dad says. "Hillary, you're some negotiator! Start high, settle for what you really wanted in the first place. Sure, Grandpa can take you driving. He taught everyone in my family, including Grandma. He's the best. Todd, stop making faces at the tuna casserole and cut up some carrots."

Questions

- Do both you and your partner work?
- How many children do you have? What are their ages?
- Do you and your partner share the household chores?
- What responsibilities do the children have?
- Are both pairs of grandparents alive?
- Do they live nearby?
- What part do they play in your family's life?

- In what ways do you run your household in the same way your parents did?
- In what ways do you run it differently?
- In what ways is your marriage like your parents', and in what ways is it different?

So for Now, Why Worry?

"Mom, it's Debbie. I got your message. I'm so glad you can stay with the children while we're gone. I've got the carpools all worked out and I'll supply the freezer, but I guess you'll want to work out your own menus. Oh, Mom, I always feel better when you and Dad can be here when we're away. You know the children so well and their routines, and you know where everything is. I'm rattling on. How are you and Dad?"

"Deb," Grandma answers, "it may just be me staying with the children."

"What?" Debbie says. "On the message machine you said both of you. Is something the matter?"

"You know Grandpa," Grandma answers. "He always feels like a fish out of water when his routine is disturbed. We had talked about staying with the children and everything seemed all right. And then this afternoon, when he came home from golf, he said something about a tournament he'd signed up for. Of course, he hadn't mentioned this tournament before. It's just like him to come up with some excuse not to do something we'd planned to do together. It's nothing new. After all these years, I should be used to it. Don't worry. With or without him, I'll be there."

"Oh, Mom, has this been happening a lot?" Debbie asks. "I know it's the reason you separated—what was it, ten years ago now? Kirk and I thought you'd worked it out and things had been better since then."

"Things were better for a long time," Grandma answers. "But the last couple of years, there have been fewer and fewer things we've done together. When we *do* do something together, we spend most of the time arguing or just not talking. That's why we canceled coming for Christmas at the last minute. We just didn't seem to be able to get along with each other, and neither of us wanted to make everyone's Christmas miserable. We thought it would be better for everybody if we stayed at home."

"Oh, Mom," Debbie says, "I'm so sorry. Todd and Hillary will miss seeing their grandpa, but I'm glad you're still coming."

"I wouldn't miss it," Grandma says. "Maybe he'll change his mind, but I doubt it. Sometimes I think it would be easier if we split up."

"Oh, don't say that!" Debbie exclaims. "You know how hard it was on Kirk and Steve when you separated the first time—and what about Hillary and Todd? They love you both so. They don't see enough of you as it is."

"Oh, Debbie, I'm sorry I upset you," Grandma says. "I never thought I'd say such a thing. But after the last couple of years, sometimes I just think we'd both be better off on our own. We've pretty much gone our separate ways as it is. For now, let's not worry about it. You've got enough on your mind. It'll probably never happen anyway. Count on me next week. Everything else—well, we'll just take things as they come."

"Mom, do you want me to talk to Kirk about Dad not coming," Debbie asks, "or do you want to tell him yourself?"

"It doesn't matter," Grandma answers. "You go ahead and tell him. Tell the children I'll see them a week from tomorrow and to make a list of anything special they want me to cook."

Questions

- How did you first hear that your parents were having trouble with their relationship?
- Were the parents yours or your partner's?

- What is your relationship like with this pair of parents? What is your partner's relationship like with them?
- What is the history of their relationship? Troubled, over the years? Good, for the most part?
- What was your first reaction to the news?
- Did you try to help the mother and/or the father work out the trouble?

No Point Worrying—When It's Done, It's Done

"Hello, Kirk. It's Dad."

"Hi, Dad," says Kirk. "Debbie told me it looks like you won't be coming next week to stay with the children. Hillary was counting on your teaching her to drive."

"Kirk, that's why I called," Grandpa says. "I'll still help Hillary learn how to drive, but it won't be next week."

"Yeah, I know," Kirk says. "Debbie said something about a golf tournament."

"Kirk," his father interrupts, "it's more than the golf tournament. Your mother and I just had a long talk. It's been overdue for both of us. We've come to the decision to get a divorce."

"A divorce!" Kirk says. "What are you talking about? Haven't we gone through this before? I thought you got this all worked out a long time ago. After all these years and all you've been through, why do it now? Isn't it a little late for all this?"

"Son, Son," Grandpa says, "that's the point. Your mother and I don't have years and years to work this out. We've tried that. Ever since we got back together, ten years ago, I think both of us have done our best to make the relationship work out. Finally, we have to accept the fact that it hasn't. The decision is ours to make. It really doesn't matter what someone else thinks about it."

"Dad," Kirk says, "have you thought about how Hillary and Todd will feel about their grandparents' getting a divorce, or how Steve and Anne's Mandy and Leslie will feel, not to mention Steve and I, and Deb and Anne? This will change everything—getting together as a family, holidays, visits. I don't know, Dad; this is really something. I think it's a mistake. You can still change your mind."

"Kirk," Grandpa says, "this has really been a hard decision for your mother and me to make, and it's been a long time coming. We didn't make it lightly, but now our minds are made up. It's final. Maybe the mistake was not making this decision a long time ago. We tried so hard to work it out for the very reasons you just mentioned. But we both know this is what's best for both of us. You and Steve, Debbie and Anne, and the children will be all right, and your mother and I are going to get on with our lives. We will need your help and understanding to do it, not questions and criticisms. It's going to be hard enough on all of us without that."

"Well," Kirk says, "this is going to take some getting used to—my own mother and father getting divorced. It's bad enough seeing people my own age breaking up. But if this is what you've decided and the decision is final, I'll do my best to help you in any way I can. How is Mom? Is she still going to feel like coming here next week?"

"Thanks, Son," Grandpa answers. "I know you will. Your Mom is doing fine—well, as fine as either of us is doing. She wouldn't consider not coming. Under the circumstances, it's probably the best thing for her to do, to get away from here for a while and have other things and other people to think about. You know, Kirk, we're as sad as you are that this is how the whole thing has come out. I guess there never is a good time for this."

"At least you had some preparation," Kirk says. "I just didn't see this coming. It may be your decision, but it sure affects all the rest of us anyway."

"I know, Son," Grandpa says. "I wish there were any other choice. We've tried everything we could think of. Please tell Hillary and Todd for me that I'll miss seeing them next week, and try to help them understand."

"Yeah," Kirk says, "I'll do my best. They'll miss you, too. Let me know what else I can do."

"Thanks, Son," Grandpa says. "And Kirk, I'm sorry it had to come out this way."

"Tell Mom we'll see her next week," Kirk says.

"I will. Good-bye, Son. I'll talk to you soon."

Questions

- How did you hear that your parents were getting a divorce?
- What was your first reaction?
- What feelings did you have?
- Was the decision mutual?
- Did they tell you the reasons why they were getting a divorce?
- Did you feel their reasons made sense? If the reasons didn't make sense to you, how did that make you feel?
- If the reasons did make sense to you, did that make you feel any better?
- Have you tried to talk them out of their decision?
- What effect do you think this decision will have on your relationship with your mother? your father?
- What effect do you think it will have on your children's relationship with their grandmother? their grandfather?
- Did you see this decision coming?

- What effects do you think the divorce will have on you? your children? your parents? your marriage?

Don't Worry... Take Action

"Kirk, it's Steve. Have you talked to Dad or Mom? What the hell is going on? I thought they'd sorted all this out a long time ago."

"Steve, I was just going to call you. I don't know what's going on. I agree with you. I don't know what to think. I thought everything was fine with them. One minute they're coming to stay with the kids while we're away, and the next thing I know only Mom's coming because Dad has a golf tournament—seemed strange to me, but we've seen stranger—then Dad calls with the 'It's over and it's final' message. I'm having a real bad time with this. In some ways I feel like I'm talking about strangers, people apart from me, not my family, distanced. At the same time, I feel like someone has just hit me in the gut. This is my mother and father, the people I love; they're a part of my life, my family. I feel so sad—all their time together, all the memories, gone. Can I fix it? How can I help? Steve, I wouldn't say this to another soul but you and Deb, but you know how I feel? I feel angry. Angry at them. Why do they have to do this, robbing the children of some sort of birthright—to have the whole picture, home, family, visits with their grandparents?"

"Kirk, I know what you mean," Steve says. "I feel the same way. I also feel like I've heard this all before. They've already done this. If they couldn't straighten themselves out ten years ago, why didn't they just end it then and get it over with? Your children were young then, and mine were barely born. They probably wouldn't have been affected as much as they will be now. They wouldn't have had the time to get used to the idea of Grandma and Grandpa as a pair."

"That's true," Kirk says. "But maybe, being older, the children will be able to understand the explanations better now than when they were younger. Speaking of which, I'm not looking forward to telling them about this. When you and I are finished talking, I guess I'll have to sit them down and try to make some sense out of this for them. That'll be a trick, since I haven't got a clue where to start, because I haven't figured it out for myself yet. You know, when you were talking, I was thinking about ten years ago. What a mess that was. Remember? All those calls late at night and early in the morning when they didn't think the other one knew about it. Mom, crying and talking about Dad, and Dad yelling and complaining about her. They sure put us through it, sticking us in the middle, trying to make us take sides with one of them against the other."

"Do I ever remember!" Steve says. "Mom really got me going there for a while. I was so angry at Dad for being unreasonable, based on all the things Mom said he'd done and was doing to her. This time, it looks like they haven't gotten into that yet. In fact, that's the eerie thing about it. They both seem so calm."

"I can take the eeriness," Kirk says. "I sure hated being in the middle between them, pulled back and forth. It seems like they're both more self-sufficient now, emotionally and financially. One of the things that worried me the most for Mom, last time, was how she was going to take care of herself. She counted on Dad for everything. Now she has her needlepoint business that keeps her busy and makes some good money, plus she just seems stronger overall than before. Maybe something good did come out of the last ten years."

"I hadn't thought of it that way," Steve says. "Maybe that's why we haven't heard the bickering and picking at each other that we used to. They've just moved into total indifference."

"Yeah," Kirk agrees. "And without an interest in each other, what they have left are just those irritating things that have always aggravated them about each other. The difference now is that instead of carrying on at each other, one just picks up and goes and plays golf, and the other designs some more needlepoint. What a life! I'm beginning to see why they would want to get a divorce. Who needs a life of aggravation? Everyone deserves more than that. Come to think of it, I think I'm going to go grab Deb, give her a big kiss, tell her to put on that slinky black dress, and take her out to celebrate how lucky we are. The kids'll love the chance to pick their favorite frozen dinner."

"Yeah," says Steve, "and you can tell Todd and Hillary that it's your own home remedy to avoid what's happening to Grandpa and Grandma."

"Great idea," Kirk laughs. "This whole thing is still going to take some getting used to. I guess a lot worse things have happened. Finally, we'll just have to learn to deal with them and move on. What do you think they'll do about where to live and things like that? Did either of them talk to you about their plans?"

"No," Steve answers. "I guess we should ask if either of them needs some help with whatever. You know, it's funny. I feel as though now I need to parent my own parents."

"I know what you mean," says Kirk. "At least there are the two of us to handle it. I think I'll suggest to Mom that she stay here for a while, since she's coming down anyway, until she and Dad can get some of this sorted out."

"Good idea," Steve says. "You know, I feel better, now that we've talked."

"So do I," Kirk agrees. "Let's keep tabs on them for a while and let each other know what's going on."

"Hey, have a great celebration!" Steve laughs.

"Right," Kirk says. "I wish everything were that easy. Talk to you later, Bro."

Questions

- Are you angry at your parents for "upsetting the apple cart"?
- Do you feel pulled between the needs of your parents? Do you feel you have to take sides?
- Do you feel you have to shoulder the emotional burdens of your mother and father?
- How were your parents behaving toward each other before their divorce decision?
- How are they treating each other now?
- In the past or present has there been "parental warfare"?
- What are your feelings about the divorce?
- How do you feel about their behavior toward each other? about their behavior toward you?
- Have you talked to other family members about the situation and your feelings?
- Have you talked to your partner about the situation and your feelings?
- In what ways can your parents' experience help you with your marital relationship?

The Ice-Cream Cone Cure

"Hillary and Todd, Mom and I have something we want to talk to you about."

"Listen, Dad," says Todd, "we've already gone over the stuff with Mom. I promise I won't tease Hillary, I'll help Grandma as much as possible..."

"Dad," Hillary breaks in, "is something wrong? I heard you talking to Uncle Steve, and you sounded upset. Has something happened to Grandma and Grandpa?"

"Grandma and Grandpa are OK, but that's what I wanted to talk to you about. They've decided to get a divorce. Your mom and I want the four of us to sort this through, talk about it and about our feelings, and discuss questions we have about it before Grandma comes next week. All of us need to help each other and them get used to the way things are now."

"Wow! They're what?" Hillary asks. "Aren't they a little old for this? Grandparents don't get divorced."

"How did it happen?" Todd asks. "Did Grandpa just wake up one morning and say, 'Hey, I think I'll get a divorce, something new and different'?"

"I don't know exactly how or when it actually happened, Todd," Dad answers. "But I do know it was a decision they made together. When Grandpa called and told me, I was as surprised as you are, and I had some of the same questions as you, Hillary. The decision is between the two of them, but all of us will have to figure out how to deal with it."

"My first thoughts were about the whole family," says Mom. "What about Christmas and all the other family get-togethers? How will this affect the rest of us? It will probably change things for us as a family, but maybe less than we think. Now that I've had more time to think about it, I've started to look at it more from their point of view—what they want in their life, and the time each of them has left to do things the way they want to and maybe to try doing some things that they wouldn't try if they stayed together."

"One thing that won't change," Dad says, "is their love for you and their interest in what you're doing and their wanting to be included in your lives. Grandpa said he was counting on teaching you to drive, Hillary, and I know he's still planning to take you fishing in the spring, Todd."

"You know, Mom and Dad," Todd says, "you make it sound OK and that everything will be fine. I guess that's true, and if this is best for them and it makes them happy, then all right. I guess I'm supposed to jump onto the bandwagon, but I have this empty feeling in my stomach. I like to think of them together. When I think of them, I think of them together. I didn't even tell Hillary this, but I was really upset that Grandpa wasn't coming, too, next week. My favorite photo is the one I have of me sitting between them on the sofa holding both their hands. Now that won't happen again."

"Todd, I think we all have that same empty feeling," Dad says. "It happens every time we lose something or something changes in our life, until we get used to the new way things are."

"It may help all of us," Mom says, "if we think about the happy times we've had together with Grandma and Grandpa, enjoy thinking about them, and then imagine some things that we can share with each of them now so that we'll have new good times to remember. After all, the four of us will be changing pretty soon, too. We're all together now, but it won't be long before Hillary goes off to school, and then Todd. Todd, you'll be away at football camp this summer. So, families are always going through changes."

"Hey," Todd says, "I hadn't thought of that. Hillary, can you skip a couple of grades and go away sooner, so that I can have your share of Rocky Road ice cream?"

"Thanks a lot," Hillary says. "Don't forget, when I'm gone, you get to do all the dishes and the garbage and the basement cleanup and..."

"OK, OK," Todd breaks in. "So I can wait for the Rocky Road. Have you considered staying back a grade? Better yet, you stay back a grade, I'll skip a grade, and we can go off together!"

"OK," Dad says, laughing, "it looks like the two of you have come to grips with Grandpa and Grandma's divorce. Now your mother and I are going out for dinner. You haven't left for college yet, so don't forget the cleanup and the garbage patrol."

Questions

- How did you tell your children about their grandparents' divorce?
- What were their reactions?
- What questions did they ask?
- What worries did your children express?
- How did you help them with those worries?
- What has been the relationship between the children and their grandparents?
- What are some ways the grandchildren can involve each grandparent in their life?
- What are some things each grandparent can do to have a closer relationship with each grandchild?

"Don't Worry 'Bout a Thing"

"Well," Kirk says, as he and his wife sit down at their table in the neighborhood restaurant, "that went a lot easier than I expected. Hillary and Todd seem to be handling this whole thing better than I am."

"They're great kids," Debbie says, unfolding her napkin and putting it in her lap. "I'm really so proud of them. They always rise to the occasion. You know, most children are a lot more resilient than we give them credit for. I'm so glad you had the idea to go out for dinner. We needed some time alone together to collect our thoughts. This has all happened so fast."

"Deb, it sure has," Kirk agrees. "For all of Mom and Dad's calmness, I can't help but think this has got to be really hard for them at their age, changing their whole life. I keep thinking about what they may need from us. Will Mom be OK financially? What about the things she's always counted on Dad physically doing for her? Can she really cope with being alone, not having someone to look after? What about balancing her checkbook? Doing her taxes? And then there's Dad. He's never cooked a meal in his life or done his own laundry. Dad's the original male chauvinist. He probably doesn't even know where the grocery store is. Financially, I don't know if they can support two separate households. Maybe we should have him come live with us. The more I think about the whole thing, the worse it all feels."

"Oh, Darling, I know how you feel," Debbie says. "I feel awful too, thinking of them alone, by themselves. It's like we're talking about each of them as though the other one has died. It's the way I felt about Mother after Dad passed away. We need to talk like this and get all our feelings out so that we can put our worst imaginings aside and be practical about what they really will need and how we can help each of them set up their new life. You know they're both so independent. Your mother might like to stay with us, though, for a while after we get back from our conference, and then your father after that. But in the long run I think they'll both want to have their own place. Maybe one or both of them will want to move down here. It would sure make it easier for us to help them that way. Then again, maybe they'll just want to stay up there where their friends are and things are familiar. They're strong and healthy. They've been doing fine up till now. That hasn't changed just because they've decided to live separately."

"You're right," Kirk says. "But I can't help feeling that for right now I need to be around to find out some of these things and help them get their lives in order. Maybe I should cancel going to the conference. You'll be there and you'll know what materials and information I'd be interested in."

"Maybe that's the best idea," Debbie says. "But before we make any decisions, let's call them and see how they're planning to do this. For all we know, they may have it all worked out and think we're nuts calling with all our concerns. Who knows, your Dad may already be teaching your Mom how to handle the money stuff, and she may be showing him how to set up his own household and make some simple recipes, too. Between us and Steve and Anne, if there are gaps, we'll get them covered."

"Who knows," Kirk laughs, "they may discover whole new interests—Mom in finances, Dad in cooking. You could be right. I'm picturing Dad right now in an apron and Mom punching a calculator. They've been so calm about this whole thing and seemed to have thought it out so thoroughly, they probably would be each other's best teacher handling the unfamiliar things. You almost wonder, if they can handle this so well, why don't they just stay together, after all? All of a sudden, I'm feeling overloaded by all of this, as though there isn't enough of me to go around. I feel pulled between the demands of our own family, of work, and of whatever needs Mom, Dad, and Steve may have because of all of this."

"Until everything gets sorted out," Debbie agrees, "it's going to be hard on all of us, but I know it's going to be the hardest on you. As close as I am to your mom and dad, they're your parents, and the divorce itself must be pulling you apart. Knowing you as I do, I'm sure you're feeling responsible for getting everything straightened out for them."

"Deb, what would I do without you?" Kirk asks. "How have I been so lucky with our relationship? Ever since I can remember, Mom and Dad's marriage has been a mess. You'd think with that as my only example, I'd mess up, too."

"Maybe seeing how hard it's been on them and how unhappy they've been," Debbie says, "you decided to have something entirely different, which caused you to act differently. You know, ever since your dad called to tell us, I've been thinking a lot about their marriage and ours. Underneath it all, I think people unconsciously decide what they want and then set out to get it. Maybe your parents wanted different things for themselves and their relationship. Who knows, maybe all the squabbling gave each of them something they wanted, and when they got tired of that there wasn't anything else to keep them together, since they're such different people and so independent. You and I wanted something else. Goodness knows, we're independent, too, but we seem to enjoy learning from each other and sharing our individuality. I don't know if any of that makes sense."

"It makes a lot of sense to me," Kirk says. "More than that, somehow something you said lifted the guilt off my shoulders. I'd been feeling that maybe I could have done something over the years to keep this from happening. Also, I wasn't feeling very good about being angry at them for doing this to all of us. That's probably why I was so stirred up about stepping in and fixing everything, thinking that if I could just get their lives sorted out, I could make up for my blaming them for causing the problem in the first place. That's got to be the most mixed-up logic I've ever heard. Talk about senseless!"

"No, it's not," Debbie says. "I understand exactly what you're saying."

"Well, if you do," Kirk says, "you're doing better than I am. One thing I do have worked out is that I can't take responsibility for their relationship or either one of their lives. I can only help them to a point; then it's up to them. Also, it's not going to help anyone if I get so involved and tied up in their stuff that everything else gets out of whack. I think that's what Dad was trying to tell me. There's another thing I'm beginning to realize. I may not like how they've handled their relationship or behaved to each other, but it's their way, not mine. They've sure helped me know what I don't want in my relationship with you, which conversely helps me know what I do want for us. I guess that's why, for me, this dinner is a celebration."

"Oh, Kirk, it *is* a celebration," Debbie says. "How we've come to have what we have, I'm not sure. I only know your mom and dad's decision has just made me more thankful for it and us."

"Maybe we should toast Mom and Dad for giving us the opportunity to see just how lucky we are!" Kirk laughs.

"Great idea," Debbie agrees. "And while we're at it, maybe we'd better order before the chef goes home."

Questions

- Do you feel your parents' divorce puts demands on you that interfere with the needs of your own family and career?
- Do you think you have to take financial responsibility for a parent?
- Do you think you will be called on to bring one of your parents into your household?
- Is your parents' divorce having a negative effect on your marriage?
- Is their divorce causing you to look more closely at your own marital relationship?
- How can you make sure that you don't allow your parents' divorce to become a permanent interruption in your own life?
- Do you feel responsible for the outcome of your parents' marriage?
- Have you discussed with your partner your feelings about your parents' divorce and the extent of your involvement with it and them during this time?

Looking at the Whole Picture

Thinking back about the episodes in this chapter, answer the following questions.

- How does the situation described in the chapter compare with your situation? What is similar? What is different?

- Have other members of your family been divorced? How did it affect you and the rest of your family?
- Comparing your own situation and the one in the chapter, whom did you identify with the most, and why? the least, and why?
- Which of the following issues are you dealing with?
  - — Your parents' emotional needs
  - — Your siblings' emotional needs
  - — Your children's emotional needs
  - — The effect of the divorce on the other parts of your life—time with your own family, your job, your free time, your outside life, and so on
  - — The effect of the divorce on you financially
  - — Feeling your loyalty divided between the two parents
  - — Your feeling of responsibility for the divorce
  - — Disillusionment with your parent(s)
  - — Your parent(s)' new relationship, if there is one
  - — Other issues
- Describe how each of these issues makes you feel.
- Whom can you talk to about these issues and your feelings?

"Every Little Thing's Gonna Be All Right"

The impact of divorce on the children of a marriage is always emotionally stunning. For people your age, it carries an additional burden. Circumstances may even dictate that you contribute financially to one or both of your parents, or that you take one of them into your own home. Even if neither of these steps is necessary, you will feel compelled, to some degree, to worry about each of your parents. You will feel responsible for shoring them up emotionally during the divorce and helping them establish new lives. This can put tremendous stress on your own family, your children and partner, and your job. It will cut into, if not eliminate, social life, free time, and peace of mind.

At the same time, somehow you need to care for your own pain at the losses and changes your parents' divorce is causing and figure out how to come to terms with them. The most important thing to remember is that, as much as you love them or as responsible as you may feel, you cannot live your parents' lives for them, nor can you expect them to live their lives as you think they should. Your ability to define the boundary between your life and theirs will determine what long-term effects their divorce will have on you, your family, and your relationship with your parents.

As demanding and difficult as this time is for you, it is not without rewarding opportunities. You can learn vital lessons from your parents' experience and build stronger, more fulfilling relationships of your own. Your respect for and acceptance of your parents' decision (if not your agreement with it) can stabilize and deepen your relationship with each of them. Confronting and responding effectively to the issues arising from the divorce can build your confidence in your own ability to handle future crises.

The divorce was your parents' decision. It is their responsibility. You cannot change or control that. You are, however, responsible for how you let the divorce affect you, and you can control your reactions to it. You decide whether to master the events in your life and move on, or be victimized by them and be permanently damaged. The choice is yours.

Summary

Main Focuses

- Fearing how your parents' divorce will complicate your life; being pulled between the needs caused by the divorce and the many demands of adulthood (family, job, friends, community, and self)
- Shifting your time and focus to be able to devote energy, money, time, and emotional strength to the needs of your parents, siblings, and your own family
- Needing to help your children cope with the crisis of their grandparents' divorce, and needing to encourage a continuing relationship between your children and their grandparents
- Feeling the need to give love and help to your parents without sacrificing the rest of the responsibilities in your life
- Using your parents' divorce as a learning tool to help strengthen your relationship with your partner and with your children

Common Concerns

- Parental warfare
- The absence of one or both parents in your life
- Your feelings of divided loyalty
- Your parents' emotional burdens
- Your parents' new relationships

Self-Esteem Exercises

- Remember, there are just so many hours in the day, and you are only one person. As obvious as this sounds, it is very easy to forget or overlook during this time.
- Make a list of your daily responsibilities, breaking them down into five categories: job, community, self, friends, and family (including parents).
- Decide how you're going to divide your time, making allowances for crisis demands as they occur.
- Plan to update this time schedule frequently to adjust to changes as they happen.
- Check in often with yourself to see how you are doing.
- Give yourself permission to let off steam in productive ways, and give yourself time-off periods to relax with your partner, with friends, with your children, or just by yourself.
- Remember, you are your own most valuable resource, and if you take care of yourself, then you'll be better able to take care of your other responsibilities.
- Appreciate yourself, knowing that you are doing the very best you can, and appreciate others as well, knowing that they are doing their very best, even though at times it's hard to see that they are.
- Remember, as important as this experience is, it is not important enough to permanently interrupt your life. **As soon as you can, come to terms with things as they now are, and get on with your own life.**

Special Section

You as an adult may discover that you are dealing with issues in current relationships that stem from issues left unresolved from the time of your or your parents' divorce. The following questions will help you determine if there has been carry-over from that experience into your present relationships.

- Do you feel safe committing yourself completely to another person?
- Do you believe a relationship can continue to be loving, supportive, and fun?
- Do you act in your marriage or intimate relationship the way your same-gender parent did? Is your behavior loving, supportive, and fun?
- Do you act unlike your same-gender parent? Why?
- Do you expect yourself to act a certain way because of how your parents acted?
- Do you expect your partner to behave in a certain way because of how your parents acted?
- Are you afraid and do you react angrily when you or your partner behaves in ways that remind you of the negative things in your parents' relationship?
- What are some specific behaviors or traits that scare and anger you?
- In what positive ways is your marital or intimate relationship like that of your parents? in what negative ways?
- How can you and your partner change these negative behaviors to make your relationship more fulfilling?

Appendix
Quick Reference Outline, by Age Group

Infancy Through Kindergarten (Ages 0–5)

Developmental Issues

1. **Egocentricity:** The child views the world as being there to support him or her; when needs are met, the child is happy; when needs are interrupted, the child is fearful and angry.
    - The child feels responsible for changes that occur.
2. **Cognitive development:** Cognitive development is limited. The child responds emotionally to what is happening around him.
3. **Trust:** Does the world feel safe and providing? "How good and lovable am I?"
4. **Autonomy:** "Is there a separation between me and the world?"
    - The child is beginning to separate from the mother and needs the father as an ally to separate.
5. **Initiative:** "When I gurgle, Mother comes."

6. **Social development:** Playtime with family members and other children occupies an important role.
   - Identification with the same-gender parent
   - Conflict: independence and self-assurance versus pleasure in and need for closeness
   - The child physically acts out feelings and needs.

Family Disruption Issues

1. Developmental issues can be weakened or strengthened by a disturbance in the family structure.
2. The child's fears about love and security mean that reassurance of love, familiar routine, consistency, physical needs, and parental emotional stability are vital.
3. Changes in or interruption of love and physical needs causes fear and anger.

Possible Feelings

- Fear, anxiety, nervousness, timidity, anger

Possible Behaviors

- Reverting to younger behaviors in the areas of toilet training, motor skills, language, eating habits, sleeping habits, stuttering, nervous habits, putting self down, social activity, resisting going to sleep, frequent waking, nightmares, returning to the bottle, resisting food, crawling instead of walking, showing less initiative, acting more passive, returning to more primitive communication, having toilet "accidents," showing signs of anxiety (clinging)
- Acting out anger: crying, tantrums, aggressive behavior toward inanimate objects, peers, adults, or self; having

new fears: the dark, heights, animals, and so forth; fretting, teeth grinding (usually this age is too young for this behavior), nail biting, refusing food or exhibiting a poor appetite, excessively increased appetite; trouble sleeping, nightmares, lethargy; and the like

Early Childhood (Ages 6–9)

Developmental Issues

1. **Cognitive development:** The child's perception of the world is beginning to move from the concrete to the more abstract:
    - The child still feels responsible for what happens in his or her environment.
    - The child still has difficulty seeing that something can be good as well as bad.
    - Events are still usually caused by something concrete.
    - There is an increased ability to understand the relationship of time and space.
    - The child identifies justice as being based on power and authority.
2. **Verbal skills:** The child begins to be able to discuss and understand.
3. **Industry versus inferiority:**
    - The child likes to feel self-sufficient and on his or her own, independent.
    - The child is eager to learn how to do things well and likes feeling competent to carry out tasks.
4. **Social development:** The world widens.

- The child has a strong sense of the family unit, but the child's focus is shifting from the family to the outside world.
- Other adults and the child's peer group have increased importance for the child.
- School is an important proving ground.

Family Disruption Issues

1. The child's strong sense of family structure and "where do I fit?"
2. The child's awareness of the interaction between other family members
3. The fear of changes in the familiar routine at home and at school
    - The child's developing imagination sets up frightening fantasies.
4. Feeling responsible for what is happening in his or her environment
5. The child's sense of well-being and security
    - The role of the father in his or her life
    - The effect on sex role development of both boys and girls
    - The child's strong sense of loss of the noncustodial parent and the familiar family picture
6. The child's feelings of mastery and independence can be undermined by the loss of the secure family base.
    - The child may feel he must take care of himself, because he cannot count on parents and family.

7. The effect of the parent(s)' emotional balance on the child
8. The effect on the child's normal developmental shift from the family to the outside world

Possible Feelings

- The child feels bad about himself or herself, shy, lost, worried, fearful, sad, angry, good or bad about school, guilty.

Possible Behaviors

- The child may have a depressive reaction instead of overt anger (behaviors: sadness, silence, withdrawal, playing alone, retreating into own room).
- The child may exhibit aggressiveness with brothers, sisters, peers, other adults.
- The child may resist visiting the other parent.
- The child may act as a parent-helper/protector because either he is called on by the parent to do so or he feels the need to do so for his parent. This role makes him feel inappropriately grown up and in charge and can create behavior problems both at home and at school.

  This role also helps the child lessen feelings of guilt but may cause him to be unwilling to take direction and may cause him to start issuing orders both at home and at school.
- The child may belittle and find fault with himself.
- The child may overperform or underachieve at school.
- The child may withdraw from activities that he or she used to enjoy.
- The child may withdraw from his or her peers.

- The child may experience nightmares, crying, bed-wetting, vomiting, fantasizing, stomach aches, headaches, trouble sleeping, nail biting.

Summary

- Worries and fears:
  - Parental warfare
  - Emotional upset of one or the other parent
  - Loss of a relationship with the parent the child is not living with
  - The involvement of a parent with a new person, especially if it's the parent the child is living with
  - Frightening possibilities
- Self-esteem issues: feeling bad about himself, feeling unlovable, unimportant
- Blaming himself

Preadolescence (Ages 10–12)

Developmental Issues

1. Family relationships and a secure family structure
2. Increased physical coordination and emotional development; improved verbal and social skills give the child a sense of independence from home and family
3. **Cognitive development:** inability to grasp a realistic understanding of the world around him
4. An expanding social world and peer relationships

- The child has a growing understanding of interpersonal relationships.
- The child seeks role models.

5. Schoolwork
6. Self-esteem
7. Puberty
   - The child's sexuality and sexual role are emerging.
   - The child is experiencing being part child, part adolescent.
   - The child experiments with clothes, make-up, smoking, drinking, and other perceived grown-up behaviors and appearances.

Family Disruption Issues

1. The child may be fearful about present conditions and future changes.
2. The child may feel his or her loyalties are divided between the two parents.
   - Conflict: love for both parents versus siding with one parent
3. The child may experience parental warfare.
4. The child may feel the loss of the noncustodial parent.
   - Self-esteem is affected: "I'm not lovable; if I'd been better..."
5. The child may develop elaborate psychological defenses to deal with emotional distress.
   - Conflict: The child may feel torn between his love for his parents and being angry at them.

- The child may convert feelings of helplessness and sadness into anger.

6. The child may feel the parent(s)' dependency on him or her.
    - Just as the child naturally is moving more into the outside world, he is pulled back by the parent(s)' needs.
    - Conflict: The child feels pulled between wanting to be with friends and helping the parent.
7. The child may feel distressed about parental dating and remarriage.
    - It's confusing to the child's emerging sexuality.
    - The child may feel that there is less time for him or her.
    - The child may feel threatened by the parent(s)' sexuality.
    - Conflict: The child's loyalty to the other parent versus "Is it OK to like this new person?"
8. The child may feel absorbed by the family conflict just when normally he is being drawn toward school and a broader social arena.

Possible Feelings

- Fear
- Feels bad about himself, guilty, sad, angry, confused, bounced back and forth between his anger and feeling bad about that anger
- Feels unloved by the parent who left and feels that this is all his or her fault

Possible Behaviors

- The child may act out anger, trying to master his or her external and internal stresses.
- The child may hide feelings and appear detached or try hard to maintain good relations with both parents.
- The child may have academic and behavior problems.
- The child may do poorly in school, exhibiting aggressive behavior toward peers, siblings.
- The child may be overly solicitous with either one or both parent(s).
- The child may take on too much responsibility.
- The child may try hard to be helpful or pleasant to cover anger or to lessen his feelings of guilt or to win love.
- The child may begin to act like the noncustodial parent, adopting his or her negative attitudes (examples: how he treats the parent he lives with; how he carries out normal household chores; acting disobedient, being stubborn, or complaining about parental guidelines).
- The child may withdraw from the things he has always enjoyed doing or things that he has always done well.
- The child may have periods of crying, nail biting, sleeping problems, headaches, stomach aches, staying at home, staying in his room, and so on.

Summary

- Fears about what is happening and what might happen: "Will I have to move? Will I stay in the same school? What will my friends think? Whom will I live with?

Where will Dad be if I am not living with him? Can I see him? How often? Where will Mom be if I am not living with her? Can I see her? How often? Am I to blame for the divorce? Do they still love me? What did I do wrong?"

Early Adolescence (Ages 13–14)

Developmental Issues

1. **New egocentrism and self-absorption:** There is an "imaginary audience" watching me all the time; everyone is watching me, reading my mind, spotting my weaknesses and flaws, and they *care* about them. The "personal fable": No one has ever... [loved, suffered, and so on] the way I do, and you don't understand me.
   - The young person feels pulled between expectations of peers and expectations of parents.
   - Identity questions: "Who am I? (what kind of family do I come from? what kind of person am I? what will I become?)"; best friends are very important and are used for feedback; the "group" is important as a mirror of the young person's self-image and how others see him or her.
2. **Cognitive development:**
   - The ability to think abstractly, to consider ideas and ideals: The young person may take an extreme position to try out his new intellectual muscle caused by his emotional need for self-assertion.
   - A shift in his or her perception of parents: The young person is beginning to see them as human but still needs for them to behave like gods.

3. **Physical development:**
   - Hormones trigger emotional ups and downs and blossoming in all directions.
   - Sexual awareness and sensitivity
4. **Social development:**
   - The young person is moving from same-gender peer groups to activities with opposite gender (feeling particularly sensitive about acceptance and belonging).
   - The young person is pulled between expectations of parents and family versus expectations of peer group: venturing out more and more, carving out a niche separate from the family, but still needing support and love from the family.
   - The young person acts out stress in alarming new ways.
5. **Emotional development:**
   - Ambivalence: Up and down; good and bad

Family Disruption Issues

1. The young person may be particularly sensitive to the disruption of his "predictable" home environment.
   - His own unpredictability makes external changes especially difficult to tolerate.
2. The young person feels loyalty to both parents.
   - He or she may feel put on the spot by such questions as "Whom do you want to live with?"
   - Parental warfare: The young person may feel as if he or she is the vehicle and the prize.
   - The young person may fantasize about the parents' getting back together.

- The young person may feel strongly the absence of the noncustodial parent.

3. The young person may respond to a confused home environment by seeking safe havens outside in friends' homes, or may "hole up" in his room to avoid the whole thing.
4. The young person may feel the loss of support and security and feel left to his own devices. He may develop independence and maturity beyond his years: "It's up to me."
5. School
   - Performing well in some activity (academic, athletic) is a normal way for this age group to define identity. It also can serve as a way for the young person to disassociate himself from his parents' problem.
6. The young person may feel the needs of the parents and the family.
   - Conflict: Self needs are at odds with parental dependency needs.
7. If the young person is experiencing confused feelings about his parents, he will not be able to look to them as the loving role models that are so necessary in helping him define his self-identity.
   - The young person needs clearly defined, loving guidelines.
8. The young person's own sexuality may be in conflict with parental dating and marrying.
   - He may feel excluded.
   - He may resist the new person's authority.
   - He may be less possessive about his parents because of his own increasing socialization (the new person may take some of the burden of the parent off the child).

Possible Feelings

- Fear of losing stability, protection, and support of the family
- Fear and anxiety about what is happening and will happen to his or her life
- Guilt: "Since I'm the center of the universe, all of this must be my fault."
- Feelings of inadequacy, being unloved
- Acute sadness about the loss of the family picture and security
- Feelings of insecurity
- Anger at both parents for not carrying out their "jobs"
- Loss of self-respect for mother and father, and adults in general
- Feeling stunned that this is happening to him or her

Possible Behaviors

- With his or her newly developed intellectual and physical prowess, the young person may respond to the situation by being aggressive verbally and physically.
- Gender-related behavior
  - Female: promiscuity, trying out extreme dressing styles, separating from the mother and resisting her authority, seductive behavior toward men in general and her father in particular
  - Male: promiscuity, hypermasculine behavior, overreacting to parental restrictions, striving for masculine identity yet lacking a real conviction about it

- Internal stress may be acted out in various ways: drinking, drug use, poor grades, reckless physical behavior, lashing out, rule breaking, truancy, performance level lower than ability, self-injury, fighting, running away.
- The young person may seek solutions outside of the home.
- This age group is less apt to take on the parents' burden than is true of younger or older age groups.

Summary

- Fears about how to mesh what is going on at home with his or her outside world: "What will my friends think? Will I have to move away from them? Will I have to stay home more? Help out more? Who is there for me? Will my parents get married again? Whom will I live with? Where will my home be?"

Middle Adolescence (Ages 15–17)

Developmental Issues

1. Ego identity (putting all the parts together)
    - For the young person's self-identity to continue to come together and grow from this stage, he or she needs to have established during the earlier developmental stages a basic sense of trust in the world around him and within himself as well as the elements of autonomy, initiative, mastery, and industry.
    - Conflict: self-absorption, looking inward (discovering his developing new self-image) versus looking outward (seeing himself compared to others and the world around him)

- Struggling with the inconsistencies between the ideal self and the real self; the ideal family and the real family; the ideal world and the real world
- Looking for a fit between the changing self and the changing society

2. Social, verbal, cognitive, physical, and emotional skills are solidifying.
   - The social radius continues to widen.
   - The movement toward independence and separation makes the young person less tolerant of parental "interference" but still dependent on that bedrock of support.
   - New boundaries are being sought and tested.
   - Emotional volatility seesaws with growing feelings of responsibility.
   - Feelings of sexuality and the need to integrate the sexual feelings into the self-image are increasing.
   - School and peers are central, but the family is still the bedrock from which to launch.

Family Disruption Issues

1. The young person may be fearful about how the family breakdown will affect his security and self-image with friends and his relationship with family members. This stage is very concerned with "How will I look?"
2. The young person may fantasize about the parents' getting back together to shore up his or her security needs.
3. The young person's struggle with self-identity may be complicated and made worse by the changes and unpredictability in the family and the household.

4. The young person either may cling more to the home front, seeking security of any sort, or may spend more time away from home, seeking security outside.
5. The young person's normally developing verbal, social, emotional, and cognitive skills may be interrupted by the family's disruption, causing him to be less mature than his peers.
6. The child may appear more mature, independent, and responsible in reaction to the family disruption.
7. The young person's feelings of responsibility toward the family and his role in the family may overbalance his needs to continue to define himself as separate though still a part of the family unit.
8. The young person may have little patience with parental warfare and may resist being pulled into the middle, because his own needs for support, love, and security are so great.
9. The young person's developing sexuality and preoccupation with his own sexuality may be at odds with having to look at his parents' sexuality in the new circumstances.
10. The young person's natural resistance to parental interference may be heightened, and the introduction of the authority of a parent's new partner may be particularly inflammatory.
11. The young person's level of trust in parents, home, institutions, and so forth may be shaken or broken by the interruption of the family's status quo.

Possible Feelings

- Fear about the changes divorce will cause around him or her and how the changes will affect his or her life and routine
- Anxiety
- Depression
- Sadness for what has been lost and what may be lost in the future: specifically, the loss of the noncustodial parent
- Anger at his parents for causing this disruption in his life conflicts with his love for his parents and his need for their support and love
- Feelings of low self-esteem: "I am unlovable," "I am not OK."
- Guilt: "What have I done?" "What am I doing?" "What can I do to make it better, make them OK?"

Possible Behaviors

- Antisocial behavior: conflicts with peers and siblings, argumentativeness, moodiness, irritability, fighting, sarcasm, anger
- Physical complaints: sleep trouble, fatigue, headaches, stomach aches, accident proneness, and so forth
- Self-destructive behavior: fast driving, substance abuse, skipping school, stealing, poor grades, promiscuity, and similar behaviors
- Changes in physical appearance
- Resistance to authority: breaking the law, failure to abide by "family rules"

- Conflict behavior:
  - Anger at one or both parents versus love
  - Loyalty to both parents versus taking sides
  - Affection for parent's new partner versus anxiety about sexuality of parent's dating relationship
  - Affection for parent's new partner versus loyalty to the parent whom the new partner is replacing
  - Wishing to be helpful to custodial parent versus the young person's need for independence
- Defensive behaviors: intellectualizing, denying, avoiding

Summary

- Your parents' battling with each other
- Your feeling of loyalty for both parents
- The loss of your noncustodial parent in your life
- Your parents' new relationships, particularly the parent with whom you live

Late Adolescence (Ages 18–19)

Developmental Issues

1. **Self-development:** The young person has strong separation and individuation urges as well as a continuing need to belong, be respected, be recognized, and be approved of.
2. **Cognitive development:** The young person has the ability to reason abstractly, plan, organize, carry things out.
3. **Physical development:** The young person has attained, or is close to attaining, full height and physical capacities.

4. **Emotional development:** The young person is well on the way toward achieving some mastery of the emotional chaos of adolescence and some degree of self-control.
5. **Social development:** The young person is able to comfortably move between the family world and the world outside, with a measure of self-identity that distinguishes him or her as being both apart from as well as a part of both groups.

Family Disruption Issues

1. The young person is confronted with his or her own separation from the family at the same time that the family is separating within itself.
2. The young person is coping with what to make of his own life as well as what to make of his family.
3. The young person is asking himself what are his own values and now what are and what will be his family's values.
4. The young person's coming to terms with his own sexuality may be confused by his parents' sexual activities with new partners.
5. The young person is confronting where he is going, what he will become, and what is happening to his family, all at the same time.

Possible Feelings

- Fear of and anxiety about how the family's disintegration will affect his or her plans for the future: "Will we have to move? Will I be able to go to school? Will I have to stay home and help out?"
- Anger at one or both parents "for doing this"

- Blaming one or the other parent for causing the break; one or both for parental bickering and other forms of "warfare" between the two parents
- Sadness for and/or anger at all the losses caused by the divorce (for example, missing the noncustodial parent)
- Guilt for causing the breakup, one parent to leave, parental bickering
- Feeling responsible for having to give one or both parents emotional support, and feeling resentful of that responsibility
- Feeling resentful of or confused by the parents' dating and remarriage

Possible Behaviors

- The young person may either withdraw into himself or herself, or act more social, academic, athletic, and the like.
- The young person may seek to be the rock of Gibraltar within the family or seek distraction in outside activities or with his peer group.
- The young person may exhibit antisocial or self-destructive behaviors: fighting, fast driving, substance abuse, sexual promiscuity, and so forth.
- The young person may attach himself to an outside source of comfort, support, love (a haven from/in the storm).
- The young person may exhibit physical effects of the crisis: accident proneness, sleep disturbances, headaches, stomach aches, skin rashes, being prone to illnesses of any sort, low-immune-system symptoms.
- The young person may stay and fight for or with the parents or leave home entirely.

Summary

- Fears about where you go from here and how the family breakup is going to affect your plans: "Can I afford to go to college? How can I get a job? Do my parents love me? Where am I going to live? Whom can I turn to when I need help? Is it up to me to make things OK? Am I smart enough, good-looking enough, popular enough, liked enough to make it?"

Early Adulthood (Ages 20–29)

Developmental Issues

1. **Emotional and physical development**
    - This is a transitional period for the young person as he or she moves from being a member of his or her original family to setting up an emotionally and physically independent unit. The young person's self-image is enhanced to the degree that he or she is financially able to be independent of parents and able to live separately from them.
    - The young person is taking responsibility for his own emotional independence.
    - The young person's living arrangements are self-contained even if finances require him to continue to live under his parents' roof.
2. **Social development**
    - The young person is looking for someone outside of himself and his family for intimacy, love, and companionship.
    - The young person's social development is carried out in three arenas: with a significant other, with his peer group, and with his circle at work. The young person's

self-esteem is enhanced to the degree that he meets his needs for inclusion, control, and intimacy in these three arenas.

3. **Intellectual development**
   - The young person is ready to make significant commitments to relationships, career/job, and personal values.
   - The young person is ready to compete mentally and take on intellectual challenges in the job setting.
   - Financial rewards enhance the young person's intellectual independence and heighten his self-regard.

Family Disruption Issues

1. The young person's need to separate from the family may be interrupted by the parents' divorce.
2. The young person's need to establish emotional and physical independence from the family may be interfered with.
3. The young person's own emotional independence may be subordinated to emotional or other needs of one or both parents.
4. The young person's earning power may be needed to help the parents.
5. Instead of being independent of the parents, the young person may be pulled back into the cross-fire between the two parents.
6. The young person's freedom to make commitments to a significant other, to a career or job, and/or to himself may be undermined.
7. The young person may develop a distrust of relationships, institutions, and conventional values.

8. The demands placed on the young person by the breakup may cause rifts in his other relationships.

Possible Feelings

- Fear of how the divorce will affect his or her life: not being able to separate and move out; not having financial support if needed or the ability to be financially independent; having to shoulder parents' emotional burden; changes and losses that are out of his control
- Anger at parents for complicating his life; at additional responsibilities for parents or siblings; at the loss of his family picture; at the changes that interfere with his plans, his lifestyle, and his ability to operate independently; at how the divorce and the parents' new relationships make him look foolish; at being pulled into his parents' warfare; at being affected by an event that is out of his control
- Sadness for the loss of his family; the familiar routines of holidays and celebrations; his role models; and so on
- Confusion about how this could have happened
- Feeling helpless to control what is happening to his parents and to himself
- Guilt for causing the breakup; for not doing something to stop the breakup; for being angry at the parents

Possible Behaviors

- The young person's loyalty to one parent may cause him or her to turn against the other.
- The young person may try to fill the gap left by the departed parent.
- The young person may take on the full emotional burden for one or both parents.

- The young person may assume part or all of the financial burden of one of the parents.
- The young person may feel responsibility for keeping the siblings intact.
- The bond among the siblings may become unusually tight.
- The young person may make changes to accommodate the new circumstances (moving back or nearer home, changing jobs, limiting his time with friends or his time at work to be available for a parent).
- The young person may use a variety of defense mechanisms to appear untouched by the breakup (disassociation, avoidance, denial, and so forth).
- The young person may turn away from both parents.
- The young person may become emotionally dependent on an outsider or an outside influence to offset the effects of the divorce.
- The young person may withhold trust or commitment from a significant other or marriage partner.

Summary

- The emotional effect on you of your parents' divorce: fear, anger, worry, sadness, guilt
- The line between your helping your parents with their needs and your need to continue to develop yourself as an independent entity
- The ability to see the difference between what has happened to your parents' relationship and what you want to make of your own life and your relationships
- The ability to look at your parents and their relationship with objectivity and compassion

- The ability to take control of your feelings, needs, and life rather than letting the crisis dictate your behavior and emotions

Adulthood (Ages 30 and Up)

Developmental Issues

1. **Physical and cognitive issues:** For the most part, these issues are served by a maintenance program that keeps you physically fit and mentally stimulated.
2. **Emotional issues:** Such issues will come up for you as changes occur in your job, in your family, in your social circle, in your primary relationship, or in your own body that place demands on you.
3. **Juggling:** You shift your resources to respond to the demands placed on you by your career, self, family, social circle, and community.

Family Disruption Issues

1. The adult may be pulled between the demands of his own family and career and the needs of his parents and siblings.
   - The breakdown may pull the adult back into his childhood family, away from his own family and career.
   - He may allow his parents' and siblings' needs to preempt the needs of his own family, friends, job, and the like.
2. The adult may see his parents' divorce affecting his own children.
3. The adult may be caught physically and emotionally in the middle between his parents.

4. The child of the divorcing parents may be manipulated into taking on the role of parent to his own parents.
5. The adult may face financial responsibility for a parent.
6. The adult may be called on to absorb one parent into his own household.
7. The adult's marriage may be tested by the emotional impact of his parents' divorce.
8. The parents' divorce may cause the child to look more closely at his own marital relationship.
9. The generational family rituals may be affected by the divorce (for example, Christmas, birthdays, holidays).
10. The ongoing nature of the adult's life may be interrupted or permanently changed as he is diverted by or pulled backward into his parents' lives.

Possible Feelings

- The adult may feel an overwhelming emotional response to the loss of his or her parental unit.
- The adult may fear how the changes in his parents' lives will affect him and his own life.
- The adult may feel anger at his parents for "upsetting the apple cart"; for what one parent has done to the other; for pulling him into the middle; for putting financial strain on him; for not living up to his expectations of what "appropriate" grandparenting role models are supposed to be; for upsetting his, the adult's, children; for taking his time away from his, the adult's, life needs; for not being able to "get their acts together"; for interrupting his life and destroying his "picture" of what life and his parents are supposed to be; for bringing a new partner into the family.

- The adult may feel anger at himself for his own thoughts and feelings toward his parents.
- The adult may feel guilty that he contributed to the divorce; that he isn't helping enough; that he feels angry at his parents.
- The adult may feel a great sadness about the losses that his parents' divorce have caused and will cause to the greater family unit (for example, the special events that can never happen again; his picture of his family as it was that now has changed) and a sadness for one or the other parent who can't cope.
- The adult may feel helpless that he was unable (1) to stop the divorce and the changes from happening; (2) to make one or both parents "OK" and whole again; (3) to cope with the ongoing demands of his family and career and the additional demands caused by the divorce.

Possible Behaviors

- The adult may withdraw into his own family and leave his parents to fend for themselves.
- The adult may actively show anger, disappointment, and disapproval toward one or both parents.
- The adult may use inappropriate ways to cope with his or her emotional confusion: drinking, substance abuse, poor job performance, aggressiveness toward mate or children, pursuing own desires regardless of his responsibilities (spending spree, promiscuity, disappearing, sports over-involvement, and so on).
- The adult may spend a disproportionate amount of time with parents or siblings.

- The adult may escape by throwing himself into his work, finding "justifiable" reasons to be away from home, to avoid his own family's needs and those of his parents.
- The adult may withdraw into himself and be unresponsive to what is going on around him.

Summary

- Fearing how the parents' divorce will complicate your life; the pull between the burden of the parents' divorce and the many demands of adulthood (family, job, friends, community, and self)
- Shifting your time and focus to devote energy, money, time, and emotional strength to the needs of your parents and siblings
- Needing to help your children cope with the crisis of their grandparents' divorce and to encourage the continuing relationship between your children and their grandparents
- Using your parents' divorce as a learning tool to help strengthen your relationship with your partner and with your children
- Feeling the need to give love and help to your parents without sacrificing the rest of the responsibilities in your own life